MATHEMATICAL PRELIMINARIES FOR COMPUTER NETWORKING

MATHEMATICAL PRELIMINARIES FOR COMPUTER NETWORKING

DAVID CLAIBORNE

A WILEY-INTERSCIENCE PUBLICATION

John Wiley & Sons, Inc.

NEW YORK / CHICHESTER / BRISBANE / TORONTO / SINGAPORE

Library of Congress Cataloging-in-Publication Data:

Claiborne, J. David.
    Mathematical preliminaries for computer networking/David Claiborne.
      p.   cm.—(Data communications and networking for computer programmers)
    Includes bibliographical references.
    1. Computer networks—Mathematics.   2. Data transmission systems—
    Mathematics.   3. Electronic digital computers—Programming.
    I. Title.   II. Series.
    TK5105.5.C54   1990   90-12302
    004.6´5—dc20   CIP
    ISBN 0-471-51062-9

CONTENTS

3

INFORMATION THEORY   44

4

GRAPH THEORY AND NETWORK FLOWS   86

BIBLIOGRAPHY   173

INDEX   176

PREFACE

Data communications and networking form one of the fastest growing areas in computing. Computer programming is a very important aspect of communications. Computer programs control all aspects of the data communication process, from encoding/encrypting the messages to managing the network to decoding/ decrypting the messages. Without computer programs to automate these operations, data communications systems could never keep up with the ever increasing traffic demands.

Computer programs manage the data communications process, allowing the communications network to operate at the maximum possible efficiency. Assessing what the maximum efficiency is and determining how to actually implement the optimal solution are mathematical problems, solved with mathematical techniques. Mathematics, particularly the theory of probability, provides the representation of the real world that enable programmers to develop, analyze, and assess coding schemes, communications protocols, and network configurations.

The mathematical techniques and methods used in communications programming are not new. Probability has its roots in France in the 1700s when Parisian gamblers began to look for ways to improve their chances of winning. Graph theory began in Switzerland in the 1800s when Euler wanted to demonstrate the number of possible routes for his evening walk. Queueing theory was used to analyze delivery schedules in the early 1900s.

But in many cases, the adaptation of existing mathematical techniques to communications problems depends on a new viewpoint or new way of applying the old methods. Shannon combined probabilistic concepts with the physics concept of entropy in 1948 and developed information theory. Information theory concepts, in turn, formed the foundation of error detection and correction. In the 1960s, Jackson introduced a method of analyzing networks of queues which became the groundwork of many developments in network design. Baskett, Chandy, Muntz, and Palacios extended Jackson's method in the early 1970s and ushered in a new wave of analysis. The recent realization of the power of trellis coding may cause many communications protocols to change because of its ability to recognize and correct errors.

Mathematical Preliminaries for Computer Networking is intended for the computer programmer who wants to understand the mathematical aspects of data communications. It is a mix of traditional techniques and novel applications, starting with the basics and gradually introducing newer and more complex topics. The book emphasizes the practical size of mathematics, using examples that relate to data communications when demonstrating the mathematical concepts.

The book is intended to be applications-oriented, not mathematically rigorous. Many mathematical theorems are introduced, and their utility is demonstrated. The theorems, however, are not proved. When possible, the techniques are introduced in a manner that facilitates future use of the techniques in computer code.

The author expresses gratitude to Gerald Cole, the series editor, for providing guidance during the writing process, to Susan Nelle for having faith that the book would be completed, and especially to his family, for providing the necessary periods of solitude.

David Claiborne

1

INTRODUCTION

WHY DATA COMMUNICATIONS PROGRAMMING?

Data communication is playing a larger and larger role in electronic data processing. As personal computers and sophisticated work stations put more computational power in the hands of end users, the importance of end users communicating with each other and with central data bases becomes more and more important. The concept of distributed processing is built on the foundation of data communication. Without reliable, efficient, and relatively inexpensive communication between the distributed processing nodes, distributed processing is not feasible.

Computer programming is a very important aspect of data communication. There are three basic reasons for this importance:

1. Processing is cheaper than expanding transmission capacity.
2. Improving transmission efficiency is cheaper than expanding transmission capacity.
3. Processing is cheaper than connect time.

These three reasons can be reduced to one general thesis. Use the power of the computers on both the transmitting and receiving ends to reduce to a bare minimum the actual information that is transmitted. This minimum must be established within constraints of accuracy and reliability.

The data processing that is done before a message is sent and after it is received can be done in the computer or work station itself or in a dedicated communications processor. Regardless of the site, the communications processor performs several functions, including

1. Message formatting and transmission.
2. Error analysis and logging of problems.
3. Support of communications protocols.
4. Encrypting and decrypting of information.
5. Routing of messages.

The efficiency with which the communications processor accomplishes each of these functions is extremely dependent on the programmer's understanding of what the communication program should accomplish and what the program is actually able to accomplish. Much study has been devoted to developing techniques that perform the functions at levels which approach the theoretical or physical limits of the network.

WHY MATHEMATICS?

Mathematics forms the theoretical foundation for analyzing, designing, and performing the functions necessary to achieve efficient, reliable, and inexpensive communication links between distributed nodes. Mathematics provides the method for reducing message information to its most elementary form, ensuring that the message requires the minimal number of bits to be passed from one point to another. Mathematics provides efficient algorithms for encoding streams of bits to ensure transmission errors can be detected and corrected to any desired level of reliability.

Mathematical techniques can be applied as communication networks are designed to analyze alternatives, determine optimal approaches, and provide realistic assessments of the final system accuracy, response time, and reliability. Once the system is operational, mathematics provides the algorithms to dynamically adjust signal strengths, bit rates, and message routing to respond to changes in network configurations and network loads.

To better understand the symbiosis between mathematics and data communication and data communication programming, consider the situation shown in Figure 1-1. Acme Manufacturing Company has five computer sites, distributed across Middleburg.

Site A, located in downtown Middleburg, is the corporate headquarters. Corporate management resides there. Sales, marketing, personnel, and accounting functions are all housed in the headquarters. Site B, on the west side, is the main factory. There the Acme Thunder is assembled from components made at smaller factories located at Sites C and D on the east side of town. Site E is the

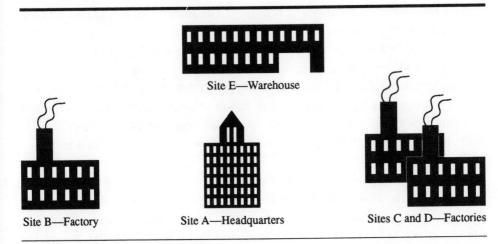

FIGURE 1-1 Acme Manufacturing.

warehouse that stores both incoming supplies and completed Acme Thunders. It is located in the new industrial park north of town.

As the company grows, it is steadily automated. Computers exist at each site to manage the functions that go on at the respective location. The headquarters computer performs all the accounting functions, including accounts receivable, accounts payable, billing, purchasing, and payroll. Each factory computer maintains work schedules and inventory requirements for scheduled Thunder units or subassemblies. The warehouse computer primarily performs an inventory function, maintaining lists of parts and completed Thunders.

Until now, each site has operated as a computational island. The only way data has moved from island to island has been via computer tapes, hand carried by Earl Lester, the company messenger. Earl picks up tapes from each site on a daily basis and delivers them to the appropriate recipients. Earl, however, is scheduled to retire in 6 months. Rather than hiring a replacement for Earl, Acme wants to link its computers.

The first consultant that Acme brought in offered a simple solution. Simply lease dedicated telephone lines from each site to every other site. To ensure redundancy, two lines would link each site. With five sites, this would result in 40 dedicated phone lines. When the Acme president saw that the annual cost of the 40 phone lines was more than he had paid Earl in the last 40 years, he decided to hire a second consultant.

The second consultant, James Carr, was both a data communication expert and a mathematician and a former programmer. He knew how to study the problem and then mathematically analyze the different options to ensure the system achieved its desired reliability and accuracy. The mathematical analysis also ensured that the cost was one that Acme could afford and that the system responsiveness would not prompt the users to recall Earl from his condo in Florida.

The first step was to analyze the amount of data generated at each site. Carr analyzed the tapes that Earl had been carrying to determine how much data was passing between each site. He also analyzed the content of the data to determine how much of it was time critical and how much could be passed overnight. Finally, he discussed Acme's growth plans to ensure that the system had sufficient expansion capability.

Carr's next step was to establish a network topology. This was done using graph theory and flow analysis. He laid a graph very similar to that of the first consultant, one that linked all sites directly with all other sites. But Carr then used his analysis of the data traffic. He found that most of the data flowed between headquarters and the other sites. He also found that the links from the factories to headquarters had sufficient capacity to allow data to flow from the warehouse through headquarters and then on to the factories and vice versa.

Using mathematical models based on graph and network theory, he simulated the network. In simulation, he found that because of the proximity of the two smaller factories, they could be linked directly with a single line to link them both back to headquarters.

With the links established, Carr looked at the time distribution of message traffic. Using queueing theory, Carr identified a potential problem on Fridays when each site would file its time card data back to payroll in headquarters. Rather than allowing a direct, interactive session between each site and headquarters, Carr proposed a system in which the time card information was entered locally, encoded into a compressed file, and then transmitted quickly to headquarters. To further alleviate the Friday backup and improve system reliability, he provided a dial-up capability between the factories and the warehouse that automatically switched in whenever the main lines got too crowded. The resulting network is shown in Figure 1-2.

As James Carr designed the Acme communication system, he used many mathematical techniques, probability, queueing theory, and network theory. The computer programs that were written to control the network and ensure system accuracy and reliability used these and more techniques, adding techniques derived from information theory and coding theory. In some instances, the mathematics is extremely detailed. Developing accurate mathematical representations of actual networks can be very tedious if not impossible. But in many instances, the mathematics can be simplified to form tractable problems that provide accurate representations.

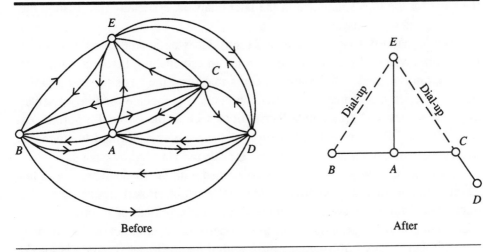

Before   After

FIGURE 1-2   Acme Manufacturing communication network.

APPROACH

The objective of this book is to introduce the mathematical techniques needed by data communication programmers. Some of the techniques can be applied in the development of actual programs used to operate data communications systems. Other techniques will allow the development of network design and configuration tools to analyze network performance with respect to response time, data accuracy and reliability, and network reliability. Finally, techniques will be introduced which, although they cannot be applied directly, will provide an understanding and appreciation of different aspects of data communication.

The book is organized into five chapters. The chapters are probability theory, information theory, graph theory and network flows, queueing theory, and selected topics. Each chapter starts with basic definitions and simple systems. As the chapter progresses, complexity is added to the systems as assumptions are eliminated. Examples drawn from data communication problems are used to illustrate real-life problem solving with the techniques introduced. Each chapter concludes with a summary and suggestions for further reading.

The theory of probability is of great practical importance to the field of data communications. Properly applied, you can use it to minimize unavoidable errors that occur when digital information is transmitted over imperfect data links. You can identify causes of errors in transmission and reception so that the inevitable errors can be detected and possibly corrected. Probability theory also forms the basis for the topics included in the later chapters, especially information theory and queueing theory.

The probability chapter (Chapter 2) introduces basic tenets and concepts of probability. Much of the chapter is devoted to establishing fundamental probability definitions and introducing concepts that form the basis for using probability theory in data communications. The concepts include random variables, expected values, and probability distributions such as the Bernoulli, normal, exponential, and Poisson. A large portion of the chapter is devoted to stochastic processes, especially processes that can be analyzed via Markov chains.

Information theory (Chapter 3) is concerned with the mathematical laws that govern the transmission and processing of information. Based on concepts introduced by Shannon in 1948, it deals with the measurement of information, the representation of information, and the capacity of communication systems to transmit and process information. Information theory forms the foundation for analyzing and implementing coding techniques that ensure accurate transmission, reduce message length, and encrypt sensitive information (but not necessarily simultaneously).

The chapter begins with the basic concepts and theorems introduced by Shannon, introducing the concept of information entropy and redundancy. These concepts are then used to develop coding techniques that maximize the entropy. The Lempel-Ziv-Welch data compression algorithm, a novel method of compressing information, is discussed in some detail. Techniques for encoding error detection and correction information into the transmitted information are provided. Finally, the chapter concludes with a discussion of data encrypting and decrypting.

Chapter 4 is devoted to graph theory and network theory. Efficient network communication depends on being able to determine the optimum link between the sender and the receiver. Many of the mathematical techniques used to determine the optimum link are based on graph theory and network theory. Graph theory also provides techniques for determining the optimum number and configuration of links to provide reliable service to a distributed network of users.

The chapter introduces the basic definitions and concepts used to describe a communication network as a graph made up of arcs and nodes. Algorithms are presented and demonstrated for determining the shortest path through a network and the maximum possible flow through the network. Both techniques are useful in designing, analyzing, and operating communication networks.

While graph theory focuses on the properties of the arcs or the links between the network nodes, queueing theory (Chapter 5) is concerned with the service performed in the nodes. Queueing theory plays a key role in the quantitative understanding of data communications networks. Queueing theory allows the concentration and buffering aspects of different network designs to be assessed prior to implementation. Queueing theory is also applied in a dynamic sense to provide optimum network performance by selecting message routing and controlling the network flow.

Queueing theory is perhaps the most difficult subject introduced. Explicit solutions to the queues formed by complex networks are generally intractable and often unsolvable. Fortunately, the approximate networks for which solutions do exist provide a good representation of the real world. With judicious simplifying assumptions, solutions can be obtained which indicate system performance, possible choke points, and underutilized processors.

The chapter begins with the simplest form of a single queue and gradually adds complexity to provide solutions to more and more general situations. A discussion of multiple queue networks as depicted in Jackson and Baskett, Muntz, Chandy, and Palacios (BMCP) networks is provided.

Chapter 6 is devoted to two additional topics, finite state machines and advanced coding techniques. In a finite state machine, each state includes a well-defined state of events. For each event, there is a corresponding action and next state defined. Events drive the machine from state to state. There must be an action and a next state defined for every event. Finite state machines are generally depicted as directed graphs in which the nodes are states and the arcs are transitions or actions. Finite state machines are widely used in the development of compilers. They form a very useful paradigm for implementing communication protocols and other aspects of data communication programming.

The chapter introduces the basic concepts of finite state machines. It discusses the interaction of states, events, actions, and state transitions. Finally, an example shows how an error checking protocol can be expressed as a finite state machine.

Cyclic redundant coding is an advanced coding technique that is widely used in modem communication, especially at higher transmission rates. Trellis coding, although first introduced in the 1960's, is now seeing widespread application. Because of its error correcting properties, trellis coding may become so pervasive that much of the communication hardware and software will have to be reworked to accommodate the technique. In Chapter 6, a brief introduction to both techniques is provided.

The level of the mathematical discussion in the book assumes a general mathematical background at the college algebra level with some knowledge of calculus. The lack of calculus, however, does not hinder the understanding in most chapters. All other mathematical principles are introduced using techniques developed in earlier chapters. For this reason, the probability chapter is particularly important. The algorithms, where presented, assume knowledge of computer programming techniques such as if-then constructions and loops.

2

PROBABILITY

The theory of probability is a formidable body of knowledge. While this body is of great mathematical interest, it also is of great practical importance to the field of data communications. Properly applied, you can use probability theory to minimize unavoidable errors that occur when digital information is transmitted over imperfect data links. It allows you to identify causes of errors in transmission and reception so that the inevitable errors can be detected and possibly corrected. Probability theory also is an indispensable tool for deducing the true lessons from network performance measurements, determining optimal network configurations, and deciding which data encoding scheme to use.

Before you can apply this formidable body on real life data communications problems, however, you must become familiar with some basic tenets and concepts. In this chapter, we will establish some fundamental probability definitions and introduce concepts that form the basis for using probability theory in data communications.

BASICS

You encounter chance phenomena daily. If you are like most people, you are very much at ease with expressions like "the chances are," "the odds are against it," and "that is impossible." Your experience is very rich with what can be called random or chance experiments. For example, toss a coin. There are two possible outcomes, heads or tails. Instinctively you know that each outcome is equally likely and should occur half the time. Toss the coin twice. Now there are four possible outcomes, heads-heads, heads-tails, tails-heads, and tails-tails. Again, you instinctively feel that each of the four outcomes is equally likely.

This coin example is easily extended to data communications. Assume you have a digital communications channel. At one end you send either 0's or 1's.

Similarly, at the other end, you receive 0's and 1's. Here again, there are four possible outcomes:

Send	Receive
0	0
0	1
1	0
1	1

The problem is the interpretation of the bits received as the correct message. If you receive a 1, can you assume a 1 was sent? If the channel is perfect with no corruption of the signal, this is a safe assumption. Similarly, if the channel is always wrong, you can safely assume the complementary value, a 0. If, however, the channel only changes the data bit sometimes, making the correct decision becomes more difficult. Indeed, there are now eight possible outcomes, as shown in Table 2-1.

TABLE 2-1   Data bits interpretation.

Outcome No.	Transmitted	Received	Assumed Transmitted
1	0	0	0 *
2	0	0	1
3	0	1	0 *
4	0	1	1
5	1	0	0
6	1	0	1 *
7	1	1	0
8	1	1	1 *

*Correctly interpreted data bit

Hopefully, the eight outcomes are not equally likely. Otherwise there is no possibility of meaningful communications. An automated coin-flipper on the receiving end would have an equal chance of receiving the correct message.

The examples of tossing the coin and the data channel are *random experiments*. They have three things in common:

1. You cannot predict beforehand how the experiment will turn out.
2. You can make a list of all possible outcomes of each experiment.

3. You have "feelings" or "beliefs" based on experience and intuition about the "likelihoods" or "probabilities" of the various outcomes.

Sample Spaces and Events

These common features of random experiments provide a basis for a mathematical model. They serve to introduce the concept of probability space and random variables. The first basic notion in probability is that of a random experiment, an experiment whose outcome cannot be determined in advance. The above examples are clearly not predictable. The second basic notion is that, although the specific outcome cannot be determined, a complete list of possible outcomes can be. This set of possible outcomes is called the *sample space*. An *event* is defined as the occurrence of one or more of the outcomes.

Going back to the data channel example, the eight points in Table 2-1 are each sample points. Taken as a whole, they comprise the sample space. An event is any combination of the outcomes. If you define an event as a correctly received message, the event consists of the sample points marked with an asterisk in the table, outcomes 1, 2, 6, and 8.

Because events are sets, the notions and notations of elementary set theory are appropriate to their discussion. If you have a sample space and an event A, the *complement* of A, A^c is the event that occurs whenever A does not occur. Also, since A and A^c can never occur at the same time, they are *disjoint events*.

If you have two events A and B, their *union* ($A \cup B$) is the event that occurs when either A or B (or both) occurs. The *intersection* of A and B ($A \cap B$) is the event during which A and B both occur. There are two special events in a sample space. The *impossible event*, the one that can never occur, is the *empty set* or *null set*. It is the set of no sample points and is often represented with the symbol $\emptyset$. The *certain event* is one that always occurs. It is the set of all the sample points. It is often represented by the symbol Ω (the Greek letter omega).

Referring to the data channel example, let event A consist of outcomes in which the assumed result is correct. Let event B consist of outcomes in which a 0 is transmitted. Combining these events in various ways yields the following results:

Event	Outcomes
A	1, 3, 6, 8
B	1, 2, 3, 4
B^c	5, 6, 7, 8
$A \cup B$	1, 2, 3, 4, 6, 8
$A \cap B$	1, 3
$\emptyset$	0
Ω	1, 2, 3, 4, 5, 6, 7, 8

Probability Measure

As stated previously, you can instinctively assign a likelihood or probability to each event in the sample space. When tossing a coin, heads and tails are intuitively assigned a probability of 1/2. Each event has an equal likelihood of occurring. In a more formal sense, this probability assignment is a *probability measure*.

A probability measure is a function that assigns a numeric value P to each event in the sample space. The probability of event A is generally denoted as $P(A)$. A probability measure must satisfy three requirements.

1. For any event A, $0 \leq P(A) \leq 1$.
2. $P(\text{sample space}) = 1$.
3. If A and B are disjoint events, then $P(A \cup B) = P(A) + P(B)$.

From this definition, several other relationships can be proven. These relationships are:

$$P(A) + P(A^c) = 1$$
$$P(\varnothing) = 0$$
$$P(A \cup B) = P(A) + P(B) - P(A \cap B)$$

In general, the probability measure assignment is based on some physical reality or observation. As noted above, the heads and tails side of the coin are instinctively assigned values of 1/2. When a coin is tossed twice, there are four possible outcomes. Continuing to assign the probability values on an intuitive basis, each outcome, HH, HT, TH, and TT, has a probability value of 1/4 associated with it.

Assigning probability values to the outcomes in the data channel example, on the other hand, is not as intuitive. It is very much a function of the data channel. It is, however, instructive to assign some arbitrary values to demonstrate the above properties. This assignment is shown in Table 2-2.

This probability meets the three requirements of a probability measure. All values are between 0 and 1. The total probability of all outcomes is 1. Also note that all outcomes are mutually disjoint. To use the example further, once again let event A consist of outcomes in which the assumed result is correct. Let event B consist of outcomes where a 0 is transmitted. Combining these events in the same ways yields the following event probabilities:

TABLE 2-2 Probability measure for data channel.

Outcome No.	Transmitted	Received	Assumed	$P(\ )$
1	0	0	0	16/32
2	0	0	1	1/32
3	0	1	0	1/32
4	0	1	1	1/32
5	1	0	0	1/32
6	1	0	1	1/32
7	1	1	0	1/32
8	1	1	1	10/32

Event	Outcomes	P(Event)
A	1, 3, 6, 8	26/32
B	1, 2, 3, 4	19/32
B^c	5, 6, 7, 8	13/32
$A \cup B$	1, 2, 3, 4, 6, 8	29/32
$A \cap B$	1, 3	16/32
$\varnothing$	0	0
Ω	1, 2, 3, 4, 5, 6, 7, 8	1

RANDOM VARIABLES

In practical applications of probability theory, it is generally more convenient to work with numbers than with outcomes such as heads or tails. If nothing else, it is easier to mathematically define functions of real numbers than functions of objects. The concept of a *random variable* allows you to do this.

> A random variable is a function X that associates a real number $X(s)$ with each outcome or point s of a sample space S. $X(s)$ is the specific value of X at the point s.

A random variable is a real-valued function defined on a sample space. Although the probability measure is also defined on the sample space, there are differences. The probability measure is defined on the set of subsets of the space. The random variable is only defined for the individual outcomes. In addition, the probability measure is restricted to values between 0 and 1. There is no such restriction on the random variable.

Because the concept of a random variable is so important to probability theory, there is standard notation used to describe the relationships between outcomes and random variables.

> The set of all outcomes s such that $X(s) = x$, where x is any specified number, is denoted $\{X(s) = a\}$. The probability of event $\{X(s) = a\}$, $P(\{X(s) = a\})$ is generally written $P(X = x)$ or $p(x)$.

You can easily extend this notation to cover other cases. For example, $(X < a)$ is the set of all outcomes s such that $X(s) < a$. In general, if E is a set of real numbers, then $(X \; in \; E)$ denotes event such that $X(s)$ is in the set E.

For a simple example, assume you toss a coin three times. Let the random variable be the number of heads that appears in the three tosses. When you toss a coin three times, there are eight possible outcomes, TTT, TTH, THT, THH, HTT, HTH, HHT, and HHH. Assuming the coin is fair, each outcome is equally likely and has a probability of 1/8. Notice that there is one outcome that produces no heads, three outcomes produce one head, three outcomes result in two heads, and one outcome results in three heads. The resulting probability function is shown graphically in Figure 2-1.

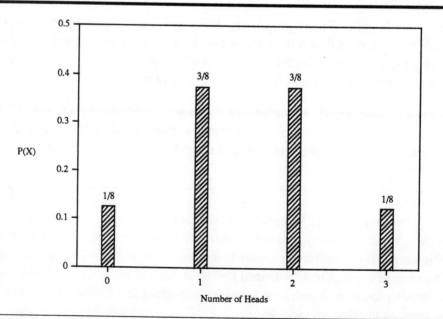

FIGURE 2-1   Probability function for number of heads in three coin tosses.

The function shown in Figure 2-1 is called a *discrete density function*. The probabilities at the possible values of the random variables represent "masses" at those values. The sum of the masses in a density function is equal to 1.

Another way to look at this three-toss example is to let X_1 be a random variable representing the number of heads on the first toss. X_1 is 1 if the result is heads, 0 if the result is tails. X_2 and X_3 are similarly defined random variables, but they represent the second and third toss results. The random variable (X_1 + X_2 + X_3) assigns to the outcomes the sum of the values that X_1, X_2, and X_3 separately assign to that point. ($X_1 + X_2 + X_3$) is a *function of the random variables X_1, X_2, and X_3*.

A function of a random variable can be any mathematical function, (X_1/X_2), $\sin(X_1)$, X_1X_2, $\log(X_1)$, etc. The new random variable may not always be well defined. For example, the square root of X_1 is only well defined if $X_1(s)$ is greater than zero for all possible outcomes s.

Up to this point, the examples of random variables have described situations in which the random variables take on a finite number of values. In the single coin toss example, the random variable has two possible values, 1 and 0. This type of random variable is a *discrete random variable*.

> A random variable X is said to be discrete if it takes on a finite or countably infinite number of distinct values. The sum of probabilities for all possible values of X is 1 in either case.

A *countably infinite set* is a set of numbers in which you know how to count up all the elements of the set without leaving any elements out, but, because the list is infinitely long, you never finish counting. The set of positive integers is the most common countably infinite set. An alternate definition for a countably infinite set is a set of numbers that you can put into a one-to-one correspondence with the set of positive integers.

An infinite set that you cannot put into a one-to-one correspondence with the set of positive integers is a *noncountably infinite set*. The set of real numbers is such a set; so is the set of all real numbers between any two specified real numbers. When a random variable has a noncountable infinite number of possible values, it is a *continuous random variable*.

> A random variable X is said to be continuous if it takes on a noncountably infinite number of distinct values and the probability that X takes any particular value is zero.

A clock provides a good example of the difference between a discrete and a continuous random variable. A digital clock has discrete values. Although the resolution of the time indicator may change from milliseconds to seconds to minutes, the times displayed are always discrete, countable values. An analog clock, with continuously moving hands, can display a noncountable infinite number of possible times.

A simple example of a continuous random variable is the *uniform distribution*. This distribution assumes that the random variable has a value between two real numbers and that it is equally likely to assume any value within that range. The probability function for a uniform distribution is defined as follows.

If the sample space S of a continuous random variable X is the interval of real numbers from a to b, and if X is uniformly distributed over the interval, the probability function of X is defined by:

$$p(x) = 0 \qquad\qquad x < a$$
$$p(x) = 1/(b - a) \qquad a \le x \le b$$
$$p(x) = 0 \qquad\qquad x > b$$

The function $p(x)$ is called the *density function* or the *probability density function*. This latter term is often abbreviated as pdf. To determine the probability that a random variable assumes a value within a specific range, you integrate the density function over that range using the equation:

$$P(c \le x \le d) \;=\; \int_{c}^{d} p(x)\, dx$$

To demonstrate these concepts, assume that the random variable is the daily high temperature on July 13 in New York City. From historical data, you can establish the range. For lack of any better information, assume that the actual value is uniformly distributed over the range. If the range is 60 degrees to 100 degrees, the resulting probability function can be depicted as in Figure 2-2.

Notice that the probability a temperature is a specific value is zero. This is a property of a continuous random variable. To determine the probability that the value lies in a specific range, integrate the probability density function. For a specific range, $80 \le x \le 90$, the probability is

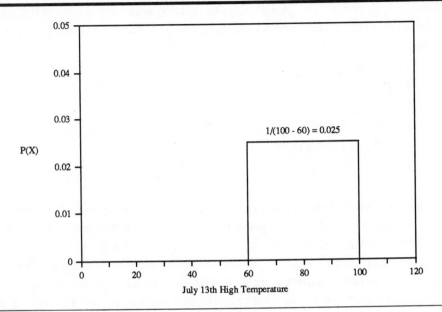

FIGURE 2-2 Uniform distribution density function.

$$P(80 \le x \le 90) \; = \; \int_{80}^{90} (1/40) \, dx = (90 - 80)(1/40) = 0.25$$

Distribution Function

We have defined the function p whose value $p(x)$ gives the probability that a random variable X will assume the value x as the density function of the random variable. Suppose that for a given random variable X you want to know the probability that X will assume a value less than or equal to x. The function that gives you this probability is called the *distribution function*. It is defined in terms of the density function p.

> The distribution function of a random variable X is the function F whose value $F(x)$ gives the probability that the random variable X will assume a value less than or equal to x.

To demonstrate this concept, once again consider the random variable X as the number of heads appearing in the three coin tosses. X has four possible values, 0, 1, 2, and 3. The probabilities associated with each value are 1/8, 3/8, 3/8, and 1/8, respectively. The distribution function, shown in Figure 2-3, is as follows:

$$F(x) = 0 \qquad\qquad \text{for } x < 0$$
$$F(x) = 1/8 \qquad\qquad \text{for } 0 \leq x < 1$$
$$F(x) = 1/8 + 3/8 = 1/2 \qquad \text{for } 1 \leq x < 2$$
$$F(x) = 1/8 + 3/8 + 3/8 = 7/8 \quad \text{for } 2 \leq x < 3$$
$$F(x) = 1 \qquad\qquad \text{for } 4 \leq x$$

The distribution function is a right continuous, nondecreasing function. For a discrete random variable X, its graph is a series of horizontal lines with vertical jumps between them at the values $x_1, x_2, \ldots, x_i, \ldots$ which X can take. The size of the first jump is $F(x_1) = p(x_1)$. The size of the ith jump ($i \geq 2$) is $F(x_i) - F(x_{i-1}) = p(x_i)$. The value of the distribution function at $-\infty$ is 0. Its value at $+\infty$ is 1.

If X is a continuous random variable, the distribution function is found by integrating the probability density function.

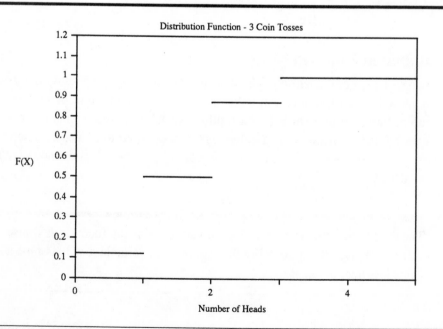

FIGURE 2-3   Distribution function for number of heads in three coin tosses.

If X is a continuous random variable for which $p(x)$ is the probability density function, the distribution function $F(x)$ is defined as:

$$F(a) = P(x \le a) = \int_{-\infty}^{a} p(x) \, dx$$

The distribution function is also called the *probability distribution function*. It is often abbreviated as PDF to distinguish it from a pdf (probability density function). Notice that, like the discrete distribution function, $F(-\infty) = 0$ and $F(+\infty) = 1$. Also, if you know the distribution function, you can differentiate it to find the density function.

For the high temperature example, the distribution function can be determined by integrating the function shown in Figure 2-2. The results, shown graphically in Figure 2-4, are as follows:

$F(x) = 0$ for $x < 60$
$F(x) = (x - 60)/(100 - 60)$ for $60 \le x < 100$
$F(x) = 1$ for $100 \ge x$

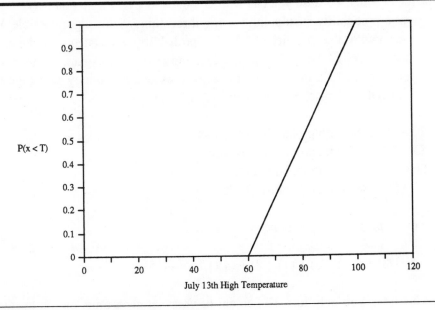

FIGURE 2-4   Uniform distribution function.

Expected Value, Mean, and Variance

One of the primary goals in the study of probability is to predict the expected outcome of a random event. In the 16th and 17th centuries, mathematicians who were also gamblers began to study games of chance to see if there was a way of predicting the value of a dice roll or a card draw. They wanted to improve their personal odds and possibly improve their expected gain. In data communications, you want to know the expected number of errors during a transmission or the expected number of service requests during a fixed time period.

Consider the following game of chance, the carnival shell game. In the game you place a coin under one of three cups. The dealer then scrambles the cups and challenges you to pick the one with the coin. If you pick the cup with the coin under it, the dealer doubles your bet. If you pick wrong, you lose your coin.

Because the dealer is very good at scrambling the cups, your choice is really a random event. You have one chance in three of doubling your coin. You have two chances of losing your coin. For each possible outcome, there is an associated money exchange. Assuming you are betting a dollar each time, you win a dollar 1/3 of the time and lose a dollar 2/3 of the time. Your *expected* win per game is $(1)(1/3) + (-1)(2/3) = -1/3$. On average, you will lose 33 cents every time you play.

In a second game, you toss three coins. You pay the house \$5 for each game. In turn, the house pays you \$3 for each head that appears. On the outset this game looks better, because you can win \$3, \$6, or \$9 every time you play.

From a probability standpoint, tossing three coins yields eight possible outcomes, each with a probability of 1/8. The probability associated with the number of heads is $p(0) = 1/8$, $p(2) = p(2) = 3/8$, and $p(3) = 1/8$. Again, for each possible outcome, 0, 1, 2, or 3 heads, there is an associated money exchange between you and the house. You can win

$0 – $5 = –$5 with probability of 1/8
$3 – $5 = –$2 with probability of 3/8
$6 – $5 = $1 with probability of 3/8
$9 – $5 = $4 with probability of 1/8

Your *expected* win per game is

$$(-5)(1/8) + (-2)(3/8) + (1)(3/8) + (4)(1/8) = -0.5$$

This time, you only lose 10 percent of your bet each time, but on average, you still can expect to lose every time you play.

The general definition of the *expected value* for a discrete random variable is as follows.

Assume a discrete sample space exists with possible outcomes w_1, w_2, ... and a probability measure P which assigns the value p_i to each w_i. If X is a random variable, the expected value of X (denoted EX) is defined to be

$$EX = X(w_1)p_1 + X(w_2)p_2 + \cdots$$

Returning to the communications example, use the above definition to determine the expected number of correct bits. To do this, first let X be a random variable whose value is 1 when the data bit is interpreted correctly. X's value is 0 when the data bit is interpreted incorrectly. A review of Table 2-2 yields the results shown in Table 2-3.

TABLE 2-3 Determining the expected number of correct bits.

Outcome #	Transmitted	Received	Assumed	x_i	p_i	$x_i p_i$
1	0	0	0	1	16/32	16/32
2	0	0	1	0	1/32	0
3	0	1	0	1	1/32	1/32
4	0	1	1	0	1/32	0
5	1	0	0	0	1/32	0
6	1	0	1	1	1/32	1/32
7	1	1	0	0	1/32	0
8	1	1	1	1	10/32	10/32
					EX	28/32

The expected number of correctly interpreted bits is 28/32 or 7/8. This result indicates an important point. Although the random variable is defined as having the discrete values of only 0 and 1, the expected value is not necessarily contained in the set of possible values. Another way of looking at the result is to say that 7 out of 8 bits should be correctly interpreted on the receiving end.

The example also demonstrates the concept of an *indicator random variable*. Let A be an event (the correct interpretation of a data bit). The random variable X_A is defined as we did above. $X_A(w)$ is 1 when the bit is correctly interpreted (w is in A). Otherwise $X_A(w)$ is 0. Because $EX_A = 1[(P(A)] + 0[P(A^C)]$, EX_A is equal to $P(A)$.

A random variable whose only values are 0 and 1 is called an *indicator random variable*.

Another way to define the expected value is in terms of a *moment about a general point a*. The definition of a moment is as follows.

Assume a discrete sample space exists with possible outcomes w_1, w_2, . . . and a probability measure P which assigns the value p_i to each w_i. Let $g(X)$ be a function of X defined as $g(X) = (x - a)^k$. The kth moment about the point a is defined to be

$$E(X - a)^k = [X(w_1) - a]^k p(x_1) + [X(w_2) - a]^k p(x) + \cdots$$

From this definition, the expected value is the first moment ($k = 1$) about zero ($a = 0$). The expected value is also called the *mean* of the distribution and is often denoted by μ (the Greek mu). The *variance*, another important moment, is defined as the second moment ($k = 2$) about the expected value ($a = EX$).

The variance is generally denoted by σ^2 (the Greek sigma squared). It tells you something about the spread, or dispersion, of the discrete random variable and about its expected value. It also provides information about the allocation of probabilities to the values of the random variables. If the values close to the expected value have the highest probabilities (or are the most probable), the variance will be relatively low. If the values at a greater distance from the expected value have higher probabilities, the variance will be larger.

Sometimes it is more convenient to work with the positive square root of the variance, that is, σ instead of σ^2. This is because the units of σ are the same as those of X. The measure σ is called the *standard deviation* of the variable X.

The relationship between the spread of the distribution about the mean and the value of variance leads to the Chebyshev inequality. It states:

For any random variable X with mean μ and variance σ^2 (both finite) and any positive integer h, the probability of getting a value that differs from the mean in one direction or the other by h standard deviations ($h\sigma$) is less than or equal to $1/h^2$.

The Chebyshev inequality is not a particularly tight measure. Its value lies in its generality. It applies to any random variable that has a mean and a variance. Nothing else needs to be known about the distribution. If more information is known about the distribution, a tighter measure often can be found.

Expected values, variances, and other moments exist for continuous random variables. They are defined in a similar fashion, using the integration of the product of the random variable and the probability density function. The general definition that applies to all moments is as follows.

Assume a continuous sample space exists with a probability density function $p(x)$. Let $g(X)$ be a function of X defined as $g(X) = (x - a)^k$. The kth moment about the point a is defined to be

$$E(X - a)^k = \int_{-\infty}^{\infty} (x - a)^k\, p(x)\, dx$$

Using this definition and the original definition of uniform distribution, the mean and variance of a uniform distribution can be easily determined. The mean is $(b + a)/2$. The variance is $(b - a)^2/12$. Notice that the two values a and b fully describe the uniform distribution. Therefore a uniform distribution is often defined as $U[a, b]$. If X is a random variable distributed uniformly from a to b, i.e., $U[a, b]$, the random variable $(X - a)/(b - a)$ is distributed uniformly from 0 to 1, i.e., $U[0, 1]$.

CONDITIONAL PROBABILITY AND INDEPENDENCE

The probability that it will rain tomorrow, given that it is raining today, is different than if it is sunny today. The chances of busting in blackjack at the start of a new deck are different than when half the cards have been played. The process of using available information to reevaluate the probability of an event is termed *conditional probability*.

Conditional probability is an important concept in probability. Like many of the previous concepts, it also is an intuitive one. The rationale is that the probability of an event may be affected by the events that preceded it.

The conditional probability of event *A*, given event *B* has occurred, is denoted as *P(A|B)*. The conditional probability is defined by the expression used to calculate its value.

The value of conditional probability is $P(A|B) = P(A \cap B)/P(B)$.

Consider the following problem. You are still playing the shell game at the carnival described earlier. You are still losing, on average, 1/3 of your bet every time you play. Finally realizing this, you are about to quit. The dealer offers to improve your chances with a slight change in the game.

Before you pick your cup, the dealer will remove one of the cups, which he guarantees is not covering your coin. You can now pick from two cups. Does the new rule make a difference? Should you continue to play?

The original probability that the coin is under any one cup is 1/3. But now you know that it is not under one of them. Assume that the coin is under cup A (event *A*) or cup B (event *B*), but that cup C was removed (event C^c because the ball is not under C). The probability you will make a correct choice is $P(A|C^c)$. $P(C^c)$ is equal to 2/3. $P(A \cap C^c)$ is equal to 1/3. Therefore $P(A|C^c)$ is 1/2. Your expected gain or loss is zero. You will not continue to lose, but you cannot win back your earlier losses.

To improve your chances further, you suggest a slight change. You will pick the cup you think is covering your coin first. Then the dealer will remove one of the other two cups, which he guarantees is not covering your coin. You can stay with your original choice or switch to the remaining one. Do these new rules make a difference? Should you stay or switch?

To state the problem, add a new event *A'*, which denotes the initial choice of cup A. Now the probability of winning if you stay with your original choice of A is the probability of event *A* given you picked A initially and the dealer removes cup B or C. This is expressed $P\{A|[A' \cap (B^c \cup C^c)]\}$. $P\{A \cap [A' \cap (B^c \cup C^c)]\}$ is 1/3. $P[A' \cap (B^c \cup C^c)]$ is 1. The probability of winning if you stay with your initial choice is 1/3.

If you switch, the probability of winning is the probability of event *B* or *C* given you picked cup A initially and the dealer removes cup C or B. This is expressed as $P\{(B \cup C)|[A' \cap (B^c \cup C^c)]\}$. $P\{(B \cup C) \cap [A' \cap (B^c \cup C^c)]\}$ is equal to 2/3. $P\{[A' \cap (B^c \cup C^c)]\}$ is equal to 1. Therefore the probability of winning if you switch is 2/3.

The best strategy is to switch. Switching actually doubles your chances of winning. Your expected win is now 33 cents per game. If the dealer lets you play for long, you can win your money back. The reason that the new strategy is better is because you know still more about the location of the coin. You know that your coin is not under the cup that is removed. You are using conditional probability.

Consider the data channel again. Continue to let event A be those outcomes in which the correct data bit is assumed and to let event B be those outcomes in which a 0 was transmitted. Using the probability measures from Table 2 and the definition of $P(A|B)$, the probability the correct data bit is assumed, given a 0 was transmitted, can be calculated.

$P(A \cap B)$ is the event consisting of outcomes 1 and 3. Because the two outcomes are disjoint, their probability is $P(1) + P(3)$, or 16/32. Similarly, event B consists of the outcomes 1, 2, 3, and 4. $P(B)$ is 19/32. Therefore $P(A|B) = 16/19$.

Similarly, you can show that the probability that the correct data bit is assumed given a 1 is transmitted is 10/13. Comparing these two conditional probability values indicates that the data channel is more likely to pass correct values for transmitted 0's than transmitted 1's.

For a third example of conditional probability, assume that you are tossing a coin four times and that the results from the first three tosses were all heads (event B). What is the probability of tossing four heads in a row (event A), i.e., the fourth toss also is heads?

It is intuitive that $P(B)$, the probability of tossing three heads in a row, is 1/8. Similarly, $P(A \cap B)$, the probability of the fourth toss also resulting in a head, is 1/16. Therefore $P(A|B)$, the conditional probability, is 1/2. This value is the same probability value as in the case in which the coin is tossed one time. In other words, when tossing a coin, the results of any toss are not affected by previous tosses. Previous information in this case does not make any difference.

This result implies that $P(A|B) = P(A)$ as long as $P(B) > 0$. Using the definition of conditional probability, this infers that $P(A \cap B) = P(A)P(B)$. When this occurs, events A and B are *independent*. Indeed, this result is used to define statistical independence of two events.

Two events, A and B, are independent if $P(A \cap B) = P(A)P(B)$.

OTHER PROBABILITY DISTRIBUTIONS

Although a probability can be any function that meets the requirements of a probability measure, many distributions have been developed which can be used to describe random experiments in the real world. The uniform distribution described earlier is one such distribution. This section describes other probability distributions that have wide application in the simulation, assessment, and management of data communications.

Binomial Distribution

A binomial trial is a very useful probabilistic process, both in theoretical probability and in data communications. First, in its simplest form, it consists of an event that has two possible outcomes. The outcomes are commonly called a success and a failure. p is the probability of a success; $(1 - p) = q$ is the probability of a failure. If, when the trial is repeated many times, each trial is independent, the series of trials is called a *Bernoulli process*. The number of successes in n trials is said to be *binomially distributed*.

The many coin toss examples used so far are Bernoulli processes. When a coin is flipped, there are two possible outcomes. Regardless of how many times you toss the coin, the probability of a heads is always the same. The probability of correctly receiving a data bit over a noisy channel is often portrayed as a Bernoulli process.

To formally define the binomial distribution, assume you have a series of n identical, independent indicator random variables, $X_1, X_2, \ldots, X_n$. X_i is equal to 1 with a probability of p and 0 with a probability of $(1 - p) = q$. If X is the sum of the n random variables, the distribution of X is a binomial distribution.

The distribution of X is:

$$P(X = k) = \frac{n!}{k!(n - k)!}\ p^k(1 - p)^{n-k}, k = 0, 1, 2, \ldots, n$$

This distribution is called the binomial distribution with parameters n and p.

Unlike the uniform distribution, the binomial distribution describes the probability of a discrete random variable. Its values are countably infinite. The behavior of P is well behaved. The probabilities increase up to the point $(n + 1)p$

and then decrease past that point. If $(n + 1)p$ happens to be a possible value of X, then there is a double maximum at $(n + 1)p - 1$ and $(n + 1)$p. Refer back to Figure 2-1 to see this behavior. When p is equal to one half, the discrete probabilities appear balanced. For values of p smaller than 1/2, the smaller values of X have larger probabilities. The converse is true when p is larger than 1/2. Figure 2-5 shows two binomial probability functions, $n = 5, p = 3/4$ and $n = 5, p = 1/4$.

The expected value of a binomial distribution is np. The variance is npq or $np(1 - p)$.

Geometric Distribution

The binomial distribution tells you how many successes you can expect in n trials. Assume you want to know how many trials it takes to achieve your first success. If X is the trial number when the first success occurs, the distribution of X is

$$P(X = k) = (1 - p)^{k-1}p, k = 1, 2, \ldots$$

This distribution is called the *geometric distribution* with parameter p.

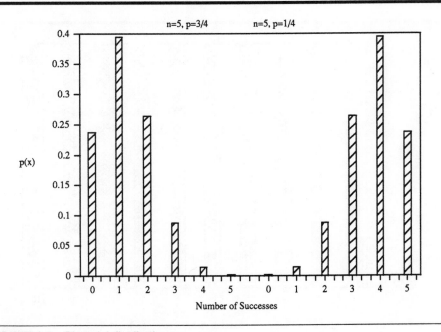

FIGURE 2-5   Binomial distributions.

Consider a communications channel. You are transmitting a message that must go through, therefore you send the same message repeatedly to ensure that it is received successfully. But you cannot afford to send the same message forever. If you know that the probability of a single successful message is p, how many times should you repeat the message to have a 95 percent probability of receiving the message correctly?

Because of the nature of the geometric distribution, all outcomes are disjoint. If the first success occurs on trial k, it cannot have occurred on $k-1$ or any previous trial nor will it occur on $k+1$ or any future trial. Therefore, the probability that the first success occurs on or before trial k is the sum of the probabilities that it occurred on all previous trials. This you should recognize as the discrete distribution function for a geometric distribution. Figure 2-6 shows the results for three different values of p, 0.2, 0.5, and 0.8. From the graph, you can see that you need to send the message 10, 4, and/or 2 times, respectively, to achieve a 90-percent probability of successful transmission.

Poisson Distribution

Suppose you are interested not in the number of successes in n trials, but in the number of successes in a finite period of time. In data communications, this could be the number of errors occurring during a transmission of a fixed-length message, or it could be the number of file requests sent to a server during a fixed

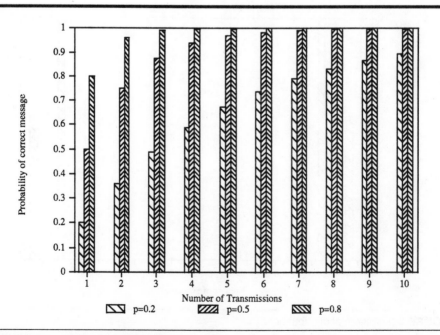

FIGURE 2-6   Geometric distribution example.

time period. Such a random variable is called a Poisson variable. The Poisson is closely related to the binomial random variable. Indeed, for certain ranges of n and p, the Poisson can be used to approximate the binomial variable. The definition of a Poisson is as follows.

A random variable X is *Poisson distributed with parameter* λ $(\lambda > 0)$ if

$$P(X = k) = \frac{\lambda^k e^{-\lambda}}{k!}, \ k = 0, 1, 2, \ldots$$

In data communications, it is generally easier to think of λ as λt, where λ is now a rate (arrivals per unit time, requests per unit time, etc.) instead of a number (arrivals, requests, etc.), and t is a unit of time. If λ is 10 requests per minute and t is 10 minutes, λt is 100 requests. In the following discussions and throughout this book, λ is a rate. Therefore, the parameter for the Poisson distribution is λt.

Consider a file server on a network. Assume that the requests for service are Poisson distributed with a $\lambda = 10$ requests per minute. The discrete probability function for the number of requests for service per minute is shown in Figure 2-7.

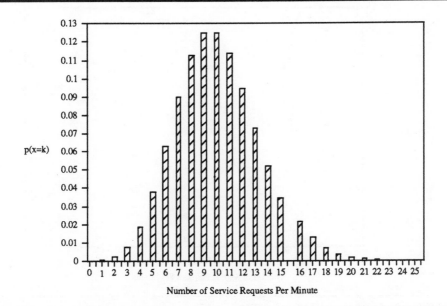

FIGURE 2-7   Poisson probability function ($\lambda = 10$).

The Poisson distribution has the property that the expected value is equal to the variance. Both are equal to λ (or λt). Therefore, for the above examples, the file server receives an average of 10 service requests per minute. The question is, what processing capacity should you install in the file server to ensure that no user is refused service because the server is too busy?

To answer the question, you need to calculate the discrete distribution function for the Poisson distribution, i.e., $P(x < k)$. This function, the sum of all $p(x)$ where $x \leq k$, can be shown to be equal to the *incomplete gamma integral*. You can find values for this integral in tables. Alternately, you can calculate the values to produce the graph shown in Figure 2-8. From this graph, the value of $P(x < 10)$ is 0.58. If you design your server capacity to process the average number of requests per minute, it is only able to keep up 58 percent of the time. If you increase the processing capacity to 15 requests per minute ($P(x < 15)$ is 0.96), your ability is much improved.

The Poisson distribution also possesses an important closure property.

Suppose $X_1, X_2, \ldots, X_n$ are mutually independent, Poisson distributed, random variables with parameters $\lambda_1, \lambda_2, \ldots, \lambda_n$. Then $X = X_1 + X_2 + \cdots + X_n$ is Poisson distributed with $\lambda = \lambda_1 + \lambda_2 + \cdots + \lambda_n$.

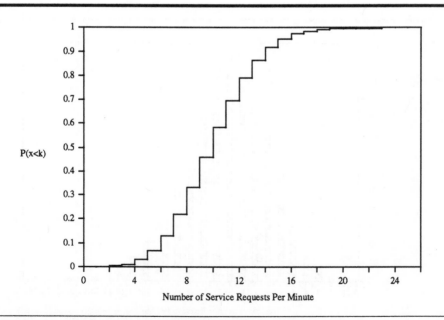

FIGURE 2-8   Poisson distribution function ($\lambda = 10$).

To demonstrate the utility of the closure property, consider the server example. Because of expansion, you want the server to also support a second network in which the average number of requests is Poisson distributed with $\lambda = 5$ per minute. Because of the closure property, the new distribution of total requests is Poisson distributed with $\lambda = 15$. If the capacity of the server is 15 requests per minute, how much does the addition of the second network degrade the ability of the server to respond to requests as they come in? How much additional processing capacity is needed to maintain the original performance level?

Figure 2-9 shows the distribution function for the server requests on the original network ($\lambda = 10$) and the new network ($\lambda = 15$). A processing capacity of 15 requests per minute allowed the original network to meet the demand more than 95 percent of the time. On the new network, however, demand is only met 57 percent of the time. To achieve the 95 percent level again, the processing capacity must be increased to process 21 or 22 requests per minute.

As stated earlier, the Poisson distribution can be used to calculate an approximation to the binomial distribution in which the value of n is large. If X is binomially distributed with parameters n and p and n is allowed to approach infinity while setting $p = \lambda/n$, X is Poisson distributed with parameter λ.

Suppose you have a binomial distribution with $n = 20$ and $p = 0.1$. This is approximately the same as a Poisson distribution with $\lambda = 2$. Table 2-4 demonstrates the closeness of the approximation.

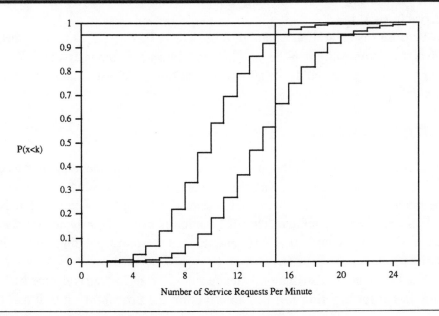

FIGURE 2-9   Poisson distribution function ($\lambda = 10$ and 15).

TABLE 2-4   Relationship between binomial distribution ($n = 20$, $p = 0.1$) and Poisson distribution ($\lambda = 2$).

Binomial Distribution		Poisson Distribution	
k	$P(x = k)$	k	$P(x = k)$
0	0.122	0	0.135
1	0.270	1	0.271
2	0.285	2	0.271
3	0.190	3	0.180
4	0.090	4	0.090
5	0.032	5	0.036
6	0.009	6	0.012
7	0.002	7	0.003
.		.	
.		.	
.		.	

Exponential Distribution

If service requests to a file server are Poisson distributed with an arrival rate of λ requests per unit time, what is the probability that no requests are received in some time interval t? From the definition of the Poisson distribution for $k = 0$, this probability is $P(N_t = 0) = e^{-\lambda t}$. Because the arrivals are independent of each other, you can extend this reasoning to show that the probability of no arrivals in interval $(t, t + s)$ is $e^{-\lambda s}$.

Because t is an arbitrary point in time, let $t = T_n$, where T_n is time of the nth arrival. The probability that the $(n + 1)^{\text{th}}$ arrival occurs in the interval $(T_n, T_n + s)$ is $1 - e^{-\lambda s}$. This result holds for all interarrival times. To state it more formally, for $n \geq 0$,

$$P(T_{n+1} - T_n \leq t \mid T_0, T_1, \ldots, T_n) = 1 - e^{-\lambda t}, t \geq 0$$

This result implies that the interarrival times are independent and identically distributed random variables, with the common distribution being $1 - e^{-\lambda t}$, $t \geq 0$. The random variables are continuous, because the number of possible arrival times is noncountably infinite. This distribution is called the *exponential distribution* with parameter λ. It is differentiable, so the corresponding probability density function is $\lambda e^{-\lambda t}$, $t \geq 0$.

The exponential distribution is memoryless. If an interarrival time has already lasted for a period t, it has no effect on the probability it will last for another s units. To state this formally, assume X is a random variable with exponential distribution. Then

$$P(X > t + s | X > t) = P(X > s), t, s \geq 0$$

The expected value of the exponential distribution is $1/\lambda$. The variance is $1/\lambda^2$. Noting that $T_n = T_1 + (T_2 - T_1) + \cdots + (T_n - T_{n-1})$, you can see that T_n is the sum of n identically distributed random variables. Because the sum of the expected values is the expected value of the sum, the expected value of T_n, the time of the nth arrival, is n/λ. Similarly, the variance of T_n is n/λ^2.

Taken together, the Poisson distribution and exponential distribution provide a set of useful tools for analyzing aspects of data communications that involve requests for service at some random time. If you assume that the requests are Poisson distributed, the only parameter you need to analyze the request rate and the distribution of request times is λ. Because the request rate is Poisson, λ is also the average request rate. You can generally either measure the average request rate from current operations or predict it.

Normal Distribution

The *normal distribution* plays a central role in the theory of probability and its applications to data communications. The normal distribution is a continuous distribution defined by its probability density function.

A random variable X is said to have a normal distribution if its probability density function is

$$f(x) = [1/(2\pi\sigma^2)^{1/2}] \exp[-(x - m)^2/2\sigma^2]$$

where m and $\sigma > 0$ are constants. The distribution is called the *normal distribution with parameters m and σ*. It is usually denoted as $N(m, \sigma^2)$.

The probability distribution function of the normal distribution is the integral of the density function. The integral, however, cannot be solved in closed form. For that reason, extensive sets of tables exist for the standard normal probability distribution function, $N(0, 1)$. A normally distributed random variable $X \{N(m, \sigma^2)\}$ can be transformed to $N(0, 1)$ by the transform $(X - m)/\sigma$.

Much of the power of the normal distribution comes from the central limit theorem. This theorem states that if $Y_1, Y_2, \ldots, Y_N$ are independent and identically distributed random variables with expected value a and variance b^2 and Z_N is the sum of $Y_1 + Y_2 + \cdots + Y_N$, then as N gets large, Z_N is normally distributed with expected value Na and variance Nb^2. This result does not depend on the distribution of Y_n if the variance b^2 is finite.

Figure 2-10 demonstrates the central limit theorem for a binomial distribution with $p = 1/2$ and $n = 10$. The points are the discrete probabilities of the number of successes equalling n. The mean value is 5 and the variance is 2.5. The solid line is the probability density function for a normal distribution with a mean of 5 and a variance of 2.5. There is very little difference between the values.

STOCHASTIC PROCESSES

Stochastic processes are phenomena that evolve as random functions of time. You encounter many empirical examples in everyday life. The daily Dow Jones industrial average over a two-year period, the number of service requests to a file server in a 24-hour period, and the number of errors over a data link during a five-minute transmission are all examples of stochastic processes.

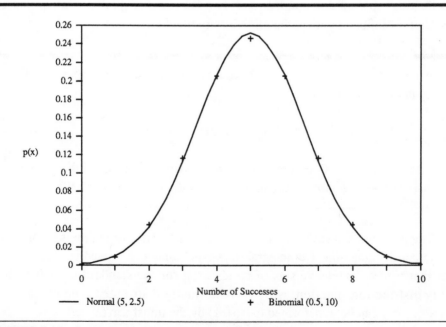

FIGURE 2-10   Comparison of normal and binomial distribution.

Mathematically, each example is described by a sequence of random variables $Z(t_1)$, $Z(t_2)$, . . . , the indices t_1, t_2, . . . , referring to the times the observations were made. When these indices vary over a discrete time set, the sequence $Z(t_i)$ is a *discrete time stochastic process*. When the chance phenomenon evolves over a continuum of times, the family of random variables $Z(t)$ is called a *continuous time stochastic process*.

Many interesting probability problems in the data communications field concern successive waiting times between recurrences of some phenomena. The waiting times between requests to a file server, the distribution of call arrival times at different nodes on a network, and the times between noise bursts on a network are all *waiting time processes*.

To make the analysis problem tractable, you usually assume that after each recurrence, the wait for the next recurrence starts anew, independent of the history of successive waiting times. Also, the probability distributions of successive waiting times are assumed to be identical.

Formally, W_1, W_2, . . . is a sequence of independent and identically distributed, nonnegative random variables. These represent successive waiting times between recurrences. Associated with the waiting times is a *counting process*, $N(t)$. $N(t)$ counts the number of recurrences that have taken place up to time t. $N(t) = 0$ for $0 \leq t < W_1$, $N(t) = 1$ for $W_1 \leq t < W_1 + W_2$, $N(t) = 2$ for $W_1 + W_2 \leq t < W_1 + W_2 + W_3$, etc.

Markov Chains

A Markov chain is a special, but very important, class of stochastic processes. A Markov chain portrays a system that can be in any one of a finite or countably infinite states, a_1, a_2, ... Y_0, Y_1, Y_2, . . . represent the states of the system at times 0, 1, 2, ... If at some time n the system is in state i, it will jump to state j according to a set of probabilities that depend on n and i. That is,

$$P(Y_{n+1} = j | Y_n = i) = p_n(i, j)$$

The key criteria is that the state at time $n + 1$ is completely determined by $p_n(i, 1)$, $p_n(i, 2)$, ... The history before time n does not affect the transition that takes place from time n to $n + 1$. In other words, where the system goes next depends only on where it is now, not how it got there.

$p_n(i, j)$ is called a transition probability. Therefore, $p_n(i, j) \geq 0$. Because a Markov chain has to go somewhere with a probability of 1, the sum of $p_n(i, j)$'s over all j's is equal to 1. If $p_n(i, j)$ is independent of n, the Markov chain is said to be *time-homogeneous*. The transition probabilities become $p(i, j)$. Time homogeneity is often assumed for computational convenience. It is customary to arrange the $p(i, j)$ into a square array. The resulting matrix is called the *transition matrix* of the Markov chain.

For a simple example, let the possible states be 0, 1, 2, 3, 4. The transition matrix is

$$
P = \begin{bmatrix}
p(0,0) & p(0,1) & p(0,2) & p(0,3) & p(0,4) \\
p(1,0) & p(1,1) & p(1,2) & p(1,3) & p(1,4) \\
p(2,0) & p(2,1) & p(2,2) & p(2,3) & p(2,4) \\
p(3,0) & p(3,1) & p(3,2) & p(3,3) & p(3,4) \\
p(4,0) & p(4,1) & p(4,2) & p(4,3) & p(4,4)
\end{bmatrix}
$$

To demonstrate some transition matrices, consider a Bernoulli process. A Bernoulli process is a sequence of binomial trials. The probability of a success at each trial is p. Let N_n be the number of successes in n trials. This is a Markov process, because the value of N_n is only dependent on the value of N_{n-1}. The transition probabilities are

$$
p(i, j) = \begin{cases}
p & \text{if } j = i + 1 \\
(1-p) & \text{if } j = i \\
0 & \text{otherwise}
\end{cases}
$$

The transition matrix is countably infinite, but the first five rows and columns are

$$
P = \begin{bmatrix}
p & 1-p & 0 & 0 & 0 \\
0 & p & 1-p & 0 & 0 \\
0 & 0 & p & 1-p & 0 \\
0 & 0 & 0 & p & 1-p \\
0 & 0 & 0 & 0 & p
\end{bmatrix}
$$

Now let T_n be the time of the nth success in a Bernoulli process. This is also a Markov chain. The transition probabilities are $p(i, j) = p(1 - p)^{j-i-1}$ if $j \geq i + 1$, 0 otherwise. The transition matrix is (again showing the first five columns and rows)

$$
P = \begin{bmatrix}
0 & p & p(1-p) & p(1-p)^2 & p(1-p)^3 \\
0 & 0 & p & p(1-p) & p(1-p)^2 \\
0 & 0 & 0 & p & p(1-p) \\
0 & 0 & 0 & 0 & p \\
0 & 0 & 0 & 0 & 0
\end{bmatrix}
$$

Visits to a Fixed State

Consider a general Markov chain $X_0, X_1, X_2, \ldots$. Let N_j be the number of times j appears in the sequence. If N_j is finite, then X eventually leaves j never to return. There is some integer n, such that $X_n = j$ and $X_m \neq j$ for $m > n$. Conversely, if N_j is infinite, then X visits j again and again. To predict the future of the process modeled by the Markov chain, it is useful to know if N_j is infinite. In this section, a number of reasonably simple criteria will be obtained in terms of the transition probabilities for determining this.

Let T_1, T_2, be the successive indices $n \geq 1$ for which $X = j$ as long as there are such n. If no such n exists ($X = j$ never occurs), T_1 and all other T's are infinite. If j only appears a finite m number of times, $T_1, T_2, \ldots, T_m$ all exist and are finite. $T_{m+1}, T_{m+2}, \ldots$, however, are again infinite.

Because of the properties of a Markov chain, starting from state i, the probability that the time interval between the $m + 1^{\text{th}}$ and m^{th} occurrence of j is $T_{m+1} - T_m = k$ is equal to the probability that the first interval $T_1 = k$ if T_m is finite. Otherwise, the probability is 0. If we define $F_k(i, j) = P_i(T_1 = k)$, F_k can be easily calculated in terms of the transition probabilities, $p(i, j)$.

$$F_k(i, j) = \begin{cases} p(i, j) & k = 1 \\ \sum p(i, b) \, F_{k-1}(b, j) & k \geq 2 \end{cases}$$

The summation is over all possible values of b except $b = j$.

Because $F_k(i, j)$ is the probability that $T_1 = k$, the sum of all F_k's over all values of k extending to infinity is equal to the probability that $T_1 < \infty$. This quantity is defined as $F(i, j)$. It is the probability that, starting at i, the Markov chain ever visits j. From the above description of $F_k(i, j)$,

$$F(i, j) = p(i, j) + \sum p(i, b) \, F_{k-1}(b, j)$$

The summation again is over all possible values of b except $b = j$. This expression can be solved, but there is a better method, as will be demonstrated.

Working again from the basic properties of a Markov chain, the probability that $N_j = m$ is $F(j, j)^{m-1}[1 - F(j, j)]$ for $m = 1, 2, \ldots$. For $i \neq j$, the probability is $1 - F(i, j)$ for $m = 0$. For $i \neq j$ and $m = 1, 2, \ldots$, the probability is $F(i, j) F(j, j)^{m-1} [1 - F(j, j)]$.

Summing these expressions over all m yields the results that the probability that $N_j < \infty$ is equal to 1 if $F(j, j) < 1$ and equal to 0 if $F(j, j) = 1$. If $N_j = \infty$ with probability 1, the expected value of N_j also is ∞. Otherwise, N_j has a geometric distribution with success probability equal to $1 - F(j, j)$. Therefore the expected value of N_j starting from state j is $1/[1 - F(j, j)]$. Similar results can be obtained for $i \neq j$.

Define $R(i, j)$ as the expected value of N_j starting from state i. The matrix R is called the *potential matrix* of the Markov chain X. From the above, $R(j, j)$ is equal to $1/[1 - F(j, j)]$ and $R(i, j)$ is equal to $F(i, j)R(j, j)$ if $i \neq j$.

These results are very important to the analysis of Markov chains. If $F(j, j) = 1$, the process will visit j an infinite number of times. Such a state j is defined as a *recurrent* state. Conversely, if $F(j, j) < 1$, the process will visit j only a finite number of times. At some point in the process there will be a final visit to j. Afterwards, j will never be visited again. In this case, j is a *transient* state.

Although the above development is based on using $F(i, j)$ to calculate $R(i, j)$, in practice the calculations are usually done in reverse order. The reason is that, in matrix notation,

$$R = I + P + P^2 + \cdots$$

I is the identity matrix, and P is the transition matrix. This expression is useful if you have the powers of the transition matrix already calculated. Alternately, you can use the relationship

$$R(I - P) = R(I - P)R = I$$

State Classifications

In dealing with Markov chains, there are many definitions that are used to classify different properties that the states and sets of states within a chain possess. Some of the more important definitions are listed below.

1. A state j is said to be *recurrent* if the probability of reaching it in a finite time is 1.
2. If there is a finite probability of never reaching state j, j is *transient*.
3. A recurrent state j is called *null* if the expected time of its first occurrence is ∞. Otherwise, state j is called *non-null*.
4. A recurrent state j is said to be *periodic with period* δ if $\delta \geq 2$ is the largest integer for which $P_j = 1$ for $T = n\delta$ and some $n \geq 1$. Otherwise, j is *aperiodic*. Recurrent, non-null, aperiodic states are called *ergodic*.
5. A set of states is said to be *closed* if no state outside of the set can be reached from any state in it.

6. If a state is a closed set by itself, the state is an *absorbing* state. State j absorbing if and only if $P(j, j) = 1$.

7. A closed set is *irreducible* if no proper subset of it is closed.

8. A Markov chain is called *irreducible* if its only closed set is the set of all states in the chain.

9. A closed subset of a Markov chain is also a Markov chain.

To demonstrate these definitions, consider the Markov chain that consists of states a, b, c, d, and e and the transition matrix

$$P = \begin{bmatrix} 1/4 & 0 & 3/4 & 0 & 0 \\ 0 & 1 & 0 & 0 & 0 \\ 0 & 0 & 2/3 & 0 & 1/3 \\ 1/2 & 1/4 & 0 & 1/4 & 0 \\ 1/3 & 0 & 1/3 & 0 & 1/3 \end{bmatrix}$$

To find the closed sets, it is useful to draw a graph with the states as vertices and directed lines from i to j if $P(i, j) > 0$. Doing that produces the graph shown in Figure 2-11.

b is an absorbing state that cannot be reached from any other state. b and d are transient states. a, c, and e are recurrent states that also form a closed set, because once any one of them is entered, the process stays in one of the three states. Overall, there are three closed sets: $\{b\}$, $\{a, c, e\}$, and $\{a, b, c, d, e\}$. Therefore, the chain is not irreducible. You can delete the rows and columns corresponding to states b and d to produce Q.

$$Q = \begin{bmatrix} 1/4 & 3/4 & 0 \\ 0 & 2/3 & 1/3 \\ 1/3 & 1/3 & 1/3 \end{bmatrix}$$

Q is a Markov chain corresponding to the closed set $\{a, c, e\}$.

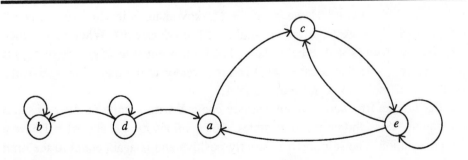

FIGURE 2-11   Transition graph.

If you relabel the states so that $a = 1$, $b = 4$, $c = 2$, $d = 5$, and $e = 3$, the transition matrix becomes

$$
P = \begin{bmatrix}
1/4 & 3/4 & 0 & 0 & 0 \\
0 & 2/3 & 1/3 & 0 & 0 \\
1/3 & 1/3 & 1/3 & 0 & 0 \\
0 & 0 & 0 & 1 & 0 \\
1/2 & 0 & 0 & 1/4 & 1/4
\end{bmatrix}
\begin{matrix}
\textbf{States} \\
a \\
c \\
e \\
b \\
d
\end{matrix}
$$

This form simplifies analysis of the Markov chain. A property of a Markov chain is that the recurrent state can be divided in a unique manner into irreducible closed sets $C_1, C_2, \ldots$ In addition to the closed set $C = C_1 \cup C_2 \cup \cdots$ of recurrent states, the chain in general will contain transient states. It is possible to go from a transient state to a recurrent state but not vice versa. On the basis of this property, you can relabel the states in an appropriate manner to put the transition matrix into the form

$$
P = \begin{bmatrix}
P_1 & 0 & 0 & . & . & . & 0 \\
0 & P_2 & 0 & . & . & . & 0 \\
0 & 0 & P_3 & . & . & . & 0 \\
. & . & . & . & . & . & . \\
. & . & . & . & . & . & . \\
. & . & . & . & . & . & . \\
Q_1 & Q_2 & Q_3 & . & . & . & Q
\end{bmatrix}
$$

$P_1, P_2, \ldots$ are the Markov matrices corresponding to the sets $C_1, C_2, \ldots$ If C is an irreducible closed set of finitely many states, then no state in C is recurrent null, and it has no transient states.

Stationary Processes

Much of the value and theory of Markov chains concerns the limiting behavior of P^m as m approaches ∞. If the chain is cycled through a large number of steps, P^m gives an indication as to how long the system will be in each state. In general, this limit need not exist. However, if the Markov chain is irreducible and aperiodic and all states are recurrent non-null, the limit does exist. When this occurs, the Markov chain is said to be *ergodic*. The limit is equal to $\pi(j)$, where $\pi(j)$ is a row vector. Note that because $\pi(j)$ is a row vector in the transition matrix, the sum of all elements in vector must equal 1.

Because an irreducible chain Markov chain X with a finite number of states has no null states and no transient states, the equations $\pi P = \pi$ and $\pi 1 = 1$ have a unique solution. The solution π is strictly positive and is again equal to the limit of P^m as m approaches ∞. A probability distribution π that satisfies $\pi = \pi P$ is called a *stationary distribution* or an *invariant distribution* for X.

To demonstrate this process, consider a Markov chain with three possible states (1, 2, and 3) and a transition matrix

$$P = \begin{bmatrix} 0.2 & 0 & 0.8 \\ 0.6 & 0.4 & 0 \\ 0.5 & 0.3 & 0.2 \end{bmatrix}$$

To find P^m, first solve for π in $\pi = \pi P$, which is

$$\pi(1) = \pi(1)0.2 + \pi(2)0.6 + \pi(3)0.5$$
$$\pi(2) = \pi(2)0.4 + \pi(3)0.3$$
$$\pi(3) = \pi(1)0.8 + \pi(3)0.2$$

This system of equation has many solutions. Using the second equation, let $\pi(2) = 30$, then $\pi(3) = 60$. From the third equation, $\pi(1) = 60$. To satisfy $\pi 1 = 1$, divide each value by $60 + 30 + 60 = 150$ to obtain $\pi = (2/5, 1/5, 2/5)$. Therefore,

$$P^\infty = \begin{bmatrix} 2/5 & 1/5 & 2/5 \\ 2/5 & 1/5 & 2/5 \\ 2/5 & 1/5 & 2/5 \end{bmatrix}$$

For a second example, consider a Markov chain with a countably infinite number of states and the transition matrix

$$P = \begin{bmatrix} q & p & 0 & 0 & 0 \\ q & 0 & p & 0 & 0 \\ & q & 0 & p & \\ & & . & . & . \\ 0 & 0 & & . & . \end{bmatrix}$$

This is one form of the *random walk* problems. A suitably disoriented person starts in state 1 and moves randomly from state to state. He moves up a level with probability p and down a level with probability q. If he is in state 1, there is a probability q that he stays in state 1.

Solving for π in $\pi = \pi P$ yields the equations

$$\pi(1) = \pi(1)q + \pi(2)p$$
$$\pi(2) = \pi(1)q + \pi(3)p$$
$$\pi(3) = \pi(2)q + \pi(4)p \cdots$$

Letting $\pi(1) = 1$ in the first equation yields $\pi(2) = p/q$. Continuing, $\pi(3) = p^2/q^2$, $\pi(4) = p^3/q^3$, and so on. Therefore, $\pi = (1, p/q, p^2/q^2, p^3/q^3, \ldots)$ is a solution for $\pi = \pi P$ as well as any other solution in the form $(c, cp/q, cp^2/q^2, cp^3/q^3, \ldots)$ for some constant c.

To get a solution, you must find a c such that the sum of the terms in π are equal to 1. If $p \geq q$, the sum is infinite for $c \neq 0$ or 0 for $c = 0$. In either case, the sum cannot be 1. Therefore no solution exists, so the limit of $P^m(i, j)$ as m approaches ∞ does not exist. On the other hand, if $p < q$, $c = 1 - p/q$ is a solution. Therefore, the limit of $P^m(i, j)$ as m approaches ∞ is $(1 - p/q)(p/q)^j$, $p < q$.

To use this result, let $q = 2p = 2/3$. The probability that the random walker is in the first state after an infinite number of steps is 1/2. The probability that he is in state 2 is 1/4. The probability that he is in state j is $(1/2)^j$.

SUMMARY

The mathematical model for a chance experiment is a probability space that consists of possible outcomes and associated *probability measures*. An *event* is some set of outcomes. Each event has an associated probability value that is between 0 and 1.

A *random variable X* is a real-valued function that associates each outcome in the probability space with a real number. The function $f_x(a) = P(X = a)$, where a varies over all possible values of X, is called the *density function* of x. The *expected value* of X is $a_1 f_x(a_1) + a_2 f_x(a_2) + \cdots$.

A *discrete random variable* has a countable or infinitely countable set of possible outcomes. A *continuous random variable* has an infinitely noncountable set of possible outcomes, and the probability that X takes on a specific value is 0. The probability that a continuous random variable lies in a specific range is found by integrating the *probability density function* over the range. An *indicator random variable* assumes only two possible values, 0 or 1.

A random variable is *uniformly distributed* over an interval if it has a probability density function that is constant over the interval and zero elsewhere.

The *distribution function* for the random variable X is defined by $F(t) = P(X \leq t)$. If X is a continuous random variable, distribution function is the integral of the probability density function. The distribution function increases from a value of $\varnothing$ at $-\infty$ to a value of 1 at $+\infty$.

The *conditional probability of A given B* is $P(A|B) = P(A \cap B)/P(B)$. It represents a reappraisal of the likelihood of event A when you know from prior information that event B has occurred. Events A and B are *independent* if $P(A \cap B) = P(A) P(B)$.

A *Bernoulli process* is a series of random experiments that have two possible outcomes, success or failure. The probability of success is p. A random variable that is equal to the number of successes in n trials is *binomially distributed* with parameters n, p where p is the probability of success in each trial. A random variable that is equal to the number of the trial when the first success occurs is *geometrically distributed* with parameter p. The number of successes in a finite time period is *Poisson distributed* with parameter λ. The time between arrivals of a Poisson process is an *exponentially distributed* continuous random variable with parameter λ.

A random variable is *normally distributed* if its probability density function is $(2\pi\sigma^2)^{-1/2} \exp -[(x - m)^2/\sigma^2]$. The special case where $m = 0$ and $\sigma = 1$ is called the *standard normal distribution*.

Stochastic processes are phenomena that evolve as random processes over time. If $W_1, W_2, \ldots$ is a sequence of independent, identically distributed, positive random variables, they serve as a model for successive *waiting times*. A *counting process* is a random step function that keeps track of the number of recurrences over a period of time.

A *Markov chain* is a special stochastic process consisting of a sequence of random variables (X_N) that have the property that the conditional distribution X_{N+1}, given $X_1, X_2, \ldots, X_N$, depends only on X_N. Where the system goes next depends only on where it is now, not on how it got there.

The primary object of interest in Markov chains is the *transition matrix P_n*, where $p_n(i, j) = P(X_{n+1} = j | X_n = i)$. Of special importance is the *time-homogeneous* case, in which the *transition probabilities* do not depend on n.

SUGGESTED READING

William Feller's *An Introduction to Probability Theory and Its Applications* was first published in 1950. Subsequent editions were released in 1957 and 1968. A second volume was added in 1962 and updated in 1971. Today, both books remain in print and form the basic foundation for many introductory probability texts and courses. The primary reason for the longevity of the volumes is Feller's ability to introduce complex topics in a manner that is both complete and understandable. If you desire additional details on any of the subjects discussed in this chapter, Feller's first volume is a very good place to start. Specifically, the axioms of discrete probability are discussed in Chapter 1. Random variables and expected values are covered in Chapters 3 and 4. Chapter 5 describes conditional probability and independence. Chapters 13 through 17 introduce the subject of stochastic processes, and Chapter 15 focuses on Markov chains with countable number of states and time-homogeneous transition matrices.

3

INFORMATION THEORY

Information theory is concerned with the mathematical laws that govern the transmission and processing of information. It deals with the measurement of information, the representation of information (i.e., encoding), and the capacity of communications systems to transmit and process information. Information theory is a very important aspect of data communications programming. It establishes the theoretical limits for the data capacity of a channel in the presence of noise. It provides the mathematical basis for the development of coding algorithms that increase the probability that the correct message is received, reduces the amount of data that has to be transmitted, and encrypts the information so it can be deciphered only by designated individuals.

Information theory is based on a simple concept of a communications system. This system, first proposed by Shannon in his 1948 landmark paper, consists of six components, as shown in Figure 3-1.

1. The *source* is where the information is generated. It sends information in the form of a *message* to the transmitter. The information can be any kind of data that is sent over a communication system.
2. The *transmitter* operates on the message in some way to make it suitable for transmission over the channel. The result is a *signal* which is passed over the channel to the receiver.
3. The *channel* is the medium used to pass the signal from the transmitter to the receiver. It can be radio waves, optical fibers, coaxial cable, etc.
4. The *noise source* is an additional signal, generally a function of the channel, which can potentially alter the transmitted signal.
5. The *receiver* performs the inverse operation of that performed by the transmitter. If the noise source has no effect on the signal, the receiver can perfectly transform the transmitted signal into a duplicate message of the original source.
6. The *destination* is the person (or thing) for whom the message and information is intended.

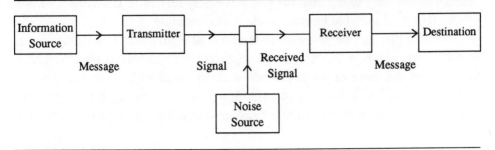

FIGURE 3-1 General communications system.

Generally, a communications system can be discrete, continuous, or a combination of the two. The discrete case is one in which both the message and the signal can be represented as symbols. Because of the textual or digital nature of most data communications, the focus of this chapter is on the discrete case.

INFORMATION ENTROPY

Two computers communicating over a telephone line via modems is a simple example of a discrete channel for transmitting information. This is a system in which a sequence of choices from a finite set of symbols can be sent from one computer to another. Each symbol will require a certain amount of time to be transmitted over the channel. The amount of time is not necessarily the same for each symbol.

Assume that the two computers are communicating in a code in which each symbol is represented by seven bits of information. There are 2^7 or 128 possible symbols. If the system communicates at 10 symbols per second, it is natural to say that the channel has a capacity of 1,280 bits per second.

This, however, does not say that information is being passed at this rate. This is the maximum possible rate. Whether or not it is obtained depends on the information source. This rationale is used to define a channel capacity, C.

> The channel capacity C is equal to the logarithm of ratio of $N(T)$ to T as T approaches infinity. $N(T)$ is the number of allowed signals in time period T.

In information theory, the logarithm function is used often. But instead of using base 10 or base e, the operation is generally performed using base 2, denoted as $\log_2$. By doing this, the result is easily related to the number of bits (binary 0 or 1) required to uniquely code the information.

For example, assume you want to send one of eight distinct messages, represented by the letters $A, B, \ldots, H$. To represent the symbols as binary signals, you need to use three digits to provide each message with a distinct code, as shown in Table 3-1. Taking the logarithm, $\log_2 8 = 3$, provides the same result. Throughout this chapter, when logarithms are referred to, the logarithm base 2 is implied.

TABLE 3-1   Binary representation of eight symbols.

Symbol	Binary Code
A	000
B	001
C	010
D	011
E	100
F	101
G	110
H	111

In a discrete communication system, the information source is a stream of symbols. Successive symbols may or may not depend on the symbols that precede them. Regardless of the dependence, you can readily portray the stream as a stochastic process, or more specifically, a Markov chain. This allows you to use the properties discussed in the previous chapter in describing the information source.

Consider a simple communication source in which the possible messages are X, Y, or Z with probabilities of occurrence of 1/2, 1/3, and 1/6, respectively. Initially, assume that the next character in the sequence is independent of the previous characters. The resulting transition matrix is

$$
P = \begin{bmatrix} 1/2 & 1/3 & 1/6 \\ 1/2 & 1/3 & 1/6 \\ 1/2 & 1/3 & 1/6 \end{bmatrix}
$$

A typical stream of characters that follow these probabilities is

XXXXYZYYYZ YXXYXXZXXX YZXYXYXYYX XXXYZYYXXY
ZXZZZYXXYY

If the symbols in the sequence have some dependence on the previous symbol, the transition matrix will not have identical rows. Assume, for example, that the same character can never appear twice in a row, but that the relative ratio remains as above. The transition matrix is now

$$P = \begin{bmatrix} 0 & 2/3 & 1/3 \\ 3/4 & 0 & 1/4 \\ 3/5 & 2/5 & 0 \end{bmatrix}$$

Using this new matrix, a typical stream of characters is

YXYXZYXYXZ YXYXYXZXYX YZXYXYZXYX YXYXZYXYXZ
XZXYXXXYZY

For the latter case, you can use the techniques from the previous chapter to solve for the stationary probabilities $\pi(j) = (9/22, 8/22, 5/22)$. If you count the occurrences of the different symbols in each string, you will see the symbols occur with approximately the expected probabilities, as shown in Table 3-2. If the sequences were extended indefinitely, the number of actual occurrences would coincide with the expected ones.

TABLE 3-2 Symbol frequencies.

Sequence	Symbol	Probability	Occurrences Expected	Actual
1	X	1/2	25.0	23
	Y	1/3	16.7	18
	Z	1/6	8.3	9
2	X	1/2	20.4	22
	Y	1/3	18.2	19
	Z	5/22	11.4	9

The two sequences of symbols are sources of information. They can be used to convey information from a source to a destination. They are obviously Markov chains. The question is, how much information is conveyed by the sequence of symbols? Does one chain convey more information than the other? Or more generally, because these are Markov chains that can continue forever, at what rate is information conveyed? To answer this question, Shannon developed a measure for information which he called *entropy*.

Suppose you have a set of possible events for which the probabilities of occurrence are $p_1, p_2, \ldots, p_n$. In addition, all the probabilities are known. The measure of information must provide insight as to how uncertain each sequential event is. More specifically, the measure, which Shannon called H, must satisfy three properties.

1. H must be continuous over the range of probabilities.
2. If all p_i are equal and $p_i = 1/n$, then H is a monotonic increasing function of n.
3. If the choice can be broken down into two successive choices, the original H should be the weighted sum of the individual values of H.

The only function that satisfies these three requirements is the weighted sum of the logarithms of the probabilities. Stated formally,

---

The entropy of a set of probabilities $p_1, p_2, \ldots, p_n$ is H where H is defined as

$$H = -\sum p_i \log p_i$$

This definition holds for any base logarithm. However, as mentioned earlier, using $\log_2$ provides some additional insights when dealing with binary events. By using $\log_2$, H is equal to the number of bits needed to encode the information contained in the process.

Consider a single Bernoulli trial with probability p of success (and q of failure). The entropy of the trial is $p \log_2 p + q \log_2 q$. If you allow the value of p to range from 0 to 1 (and q from 1 to 0), the entropy of the trial forms an inverted parabola, as shown in Figure 3-2.

The curve indicates several important properties of the information entropy function. First, if the probability of an event in a process is unity ($p = 1$ or $q = 1$), it has to happen. The fact that it does happen does not convey any information. Also, by the rules of probability measure, if the probability of one event is unity, the probability of all other events is zero. Stated more formally, H is equal to 0 if and only if one probability in the process has a value of unity and all other probabilities are zero.

The maximum entropy occurs when $p = q = 1/2$. If the number of possible events in the process is n, then the maximum value of H occurs when all events are equally likely with a probability of $1/n$. This maximum entropy value is $n(1/n \log_2 n) = \log_2 n$. Intuitively, this is the most uncertain situation.

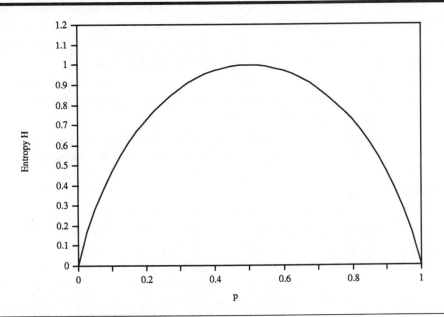

FIGURE 3-2   Entropy of a single Bernoulli trial.

Four other useful properties of the entropy function can be derived from the initial definition.

1. The entropy of a joint event, $H(x, y)$ is less than or equal to the sum of the individual entropies, $H(x) + H(y)$.
2. Any change in the probabilities of a process that makes the probabilities more equal increases the entropy of the process.
3. The entropy of a joint event, $H(x, y)$, is the entropy of x, $H(x)$, plus the entropy of y when x is known, $H_x(y)$.
4. The entropy of y is never increased by the knowledge of x.

Consider again the two Markov processes to generate the symbols X, Y, and Z. Because each of these represents a random source of information, you should be able to calculate the entropy of each source.

In the first case, in which the symbols are independent of each other, H is simple, $-\sum p_i \log_2 p_i$. For the above case, H is $-[1/2 \log_2 1/2 + 1/3 \log_2 (1/3) + 1/6 \log_2 (1/6)] = 1.459$. Based on this result it will take 1.459 bits to send each symbol. Also, if the symbols arrive at 10 symbols per second, the information will pass at 14.59 bits per second.

When the symbols are not independent of each other, as in the second case, you have an entropy H_i for each state i. The entropy of the source H is defined as the average over time of all the H_i, weighted in accordance with their probability of occurrence. In general, this can be very hard to calculate. If, however, the process is stationary and the stationary probabilities are known (i.e., P^m as m approaches infinity), H is calculated as with the independent variables, but using the stationary probabilities for each event.

For the second case, H is $-[9/22 \log_2 9/22 + 8/22 \log_2 (8/22) + 5/22 \log_2 (5/22)] = 1.544$. Notice that this process contains more information than the first process. Therefore it requires slightly more bits to send the information over a channel.

If all three symbols are equally likely and independent, the entropy of the source is a maximum. In this case H is $\log_2 3 = 1.585$. Again notice that this value is greater than that of the two previous sources, but only slightly.

The ratio of entropy of a source to maximum possible entropy is defined as *relative entropy*. For the first source, the relative entropy of source A is $1.459/1.585 = 0.920$. The second source has relative entropy of $1.544/1.585 = .974$. Another useful quantity is the *redundancy of a source*, defined as $1 -$ relative entropy. The redundancy of the two sources is 0.080 and 0.026, respectively.

The English language has been studied extensively to determine its redundancy. When considering statistical structure over eight or fewer letters, English text is approximately 50 percent redundant. This fact can be used advantageously to develop coding schemes that efficiently transmit coded text.

Another interesting aspect of language redundancy is its relationship to crossword puzzles. If text has no redundancy, any sequence of text has a reasonable meaning as well as any two-dimensional text. If a language has zero redundancy, all crossword puzzles become trivial, because all letter combinations have meaning. On the other hand, if the redundancy of a language gets too high, too many constraints are placed on the language to make a crossword puzzle possible. Consider pig Latin, in which all words end in "ay." The "ay" ending makes the language redundant and makes construction of a crossword puzzle impossible.

A detailed analysis shows that if the constraints imposed by the language are chaotic and random, large crossword puzzles are just possible when the redundancy is 50 percent. If the redundancy is 33 percent, three-dimensional crossword puzzles are possible.

Fundamental Theorem for a Noiseless Channel

In the previous examples, H, the entropy of a source, has been interpreted as the rate that information is generated by the source. The fundamental theorem for a noiseless channel justifies this interpretation. The theorem states that H determines the channel capacity for most efficient coding.

To demonstrate this theorem, consider a source that generates four symbols, $A, B, C,$ and D with probabilities 1/2, 1/4, 1/8, and 1/8. The sequence of successive symbols is independent. The entropy of this source is 7/4 bits per symbol. If the four symbols were equally likely, the entropy would be two bits per symbol. Therefore the relative entropy of the source is 7/8.

To send these symbols over a binary channel (0's or 1's only), use the following coding scheme:

A 00
B 01
C 10
D 11

This coding scheme uses two bits per symbol. On average, the result is the same, two bits per symbol. If the channel is capable of supporting 1,000 bits per second, you can send the information at 500 symbols per second. However, because H is only 7/4 bits per symbol, you are sending only 875 bits of information per second. You are using only 87.5 percent of the channel's capacity.

The inability of the coding scheme to achieve the full channel capacity arises because the two-bit per symbol coding scheme is optimum only when the symbols are equally likely. According to the noiseless channel theorem, you should be able to develop a coding scheme that allows full use of the channel.

Consider the following scheme:

A 0
B 10
C 110
D 111

This scheme uses a technique known as *Huffman coding*. The technique itself will be explained later in the chapter. The basis of the technique is to let the symbols with higher probabilities require fewer bits to encode and transmit. This should reduce the average bits per symbol.

In this case it does, because the average number of bits per symbol with the new coding scheme is 7/4 bits per symbol. Transmitting over the channel at 1,000 bits per second now allows the transmission of 571 symbols per second. Because each symbol contains 7/4 bits of information, the information transfer rate is 1,000 bits per second. With the new coding scheme, you can utilize the full capacity of the channel for information transfer.

Another way to examine the coding schemes is to determine the probability that a 0 or 1 appears in the two schemes. The binary numbers 0 and 1 are indicator random variables in a sequence. As such, their probability is equal to their expected value. In the first scheme, the expected number of times a 0 appears (on a per symbol basis) is $2(1/2) + 1(1/4) + 1(1/8) + 0(1/8) = 11/8$. Because the coding scheme sends two bits per symbol, the expected number of 0's on a per bit basis is 11/16. A similar calculation shows that the probability of a 1 is 5/8. The entropy of the binary sequence of 0's and 1's is 0.896 bits per coded symbol.

In the second scheme, the expected number of 0's is $1(1/2) + 1(1/4) + 1/8(1) + 0(1/8) = 7/8$. The expected number of 1's is $0(1/2) + 1(1/4) + 1/8(2) + 1/8(3) = 7/8$. In this scheme, the number of bits per symbol is 7/4. Therefore both probabilities are equal to 1/2. The entropy of the second sequence is one bit per coded symbol, the maximum possible entropy value.

This example demonstrates an important point. You started with a sequence of symbols $A, B, C,$ and D, whose probabilities were such that the process has a relative entropy of 7/8. Brute force coding produces an encoding scheme that uses only 87.5 percent of the channel capacity. But by using techniques based on the information content of each symbol, you can develop a coding scheme that compensates for redundancy in the original process and allows full utilization of the channel. This elimination of redundancy by encoding the source is termed *data compression.*

To state the noiseless channel theorem in another way, any sequence of symbols can be encoded to reduce redundancy to an arbitrarily small number. With proper encoding, the channel utilization can be enhanced so that it is arbitrarily close to 100 percent. In practice, however, this often results in extremely long codes (strings of binary bits associated with a discrete symbol or group of symbols). When the channel is noiseless, the length of the code does not affect the probability that it is received correctly. When noise is injected, there must be some tradeoff between the noise on the channel and the length of the codes.

DISCRETE CHANNEL WITH NOISE

A noisy channel is one fed by two sources, noise and signal. Both the noise and signal are statistical processes. Let $H(x)$ be the entropy of the source and $H(y)$ be the entropy of the received signal. If the channel is noiseless, $H(x) = H(y)$. The joint entropy $H(x, y)$ is equal to $H(x) + H_x(y)$.

In the real world, all channels have noise. If a channel is noisy, it is not possible to reconstruct the original signal with certainty. There are, however, ways to reconstruct the signal so that the effects of the noise are minimized for the given circumstances.

Consider a binary source that is transmitting 1,000 0's or 1's per second. The probabilities of the two symbols are both equal to 1/2. Therefore, the source is generating information at 1,000 bits per second. Now, because of a noisy channel, 1 in 100 of the signals is received incorrectly. What is the new rate of information transmission?

The first answer that comes to mind is 990 bits per second, reflecting that 99 out of 100 bits are received correctly. If you carry this reasoning to its extreme case, you can see its fallacy. Consider the case in which the channel is so noisy that the received signal is independent of the transmitted signal. In this case, the probability of correctly interpreting the received signal is 1/2. The number of correct bits received is 500 bits per second. But how do you tell which bit is right and which is wrong? The best scheme for interpreting the received signal is to assume that all 1's are sent or all 0's. By doing this, you will be right half the time. You do not, however, receive any information.

The proper reduction to make to the information transfer rate is the amount of information that is missing in the received signal. This can be thought of as the uncertainty you have about the result that you received. This is, in effect, the conditional entropy of the signal given the noise, $H_y(x)$, often called the *equivocation*. The actual transmission rate is $R = H(x) - H_y(x)$.

Continuing with the example, $H_y(x)$ is calculated from the conditional probabilities that if a 0 (or 1) is received, a 0 or 1 was sent. If a 0 is received, the probability that a 0 was sent is 0.99. The probability that a 1 was sent is 0.01. Therefore $H_y(x)$ is $-(0.99 \log_2 0.99 + 0.01 \log_2 0.01) = 0.081$ bits per symbol or 81 bits per second. The system has a transmission rate of $1,000 - 81 = 919$ bits per second.

If you know when the errors occur, it is possible to correct them. Consider that as the information is sent over the noisy channel, it is watched by an omniscient bit minder. The bit minder notes whenever an error occurs and sends a signal to the receiver that the last bit was wrong and should be changed. The channel the bit minder uses is called the *correction channel*.

Still continuing with the current example, the bit minder sends a continuous stream of information over the correction channel. The bit minder is, in effect, an information source that sends 1's 99 percent of the time, indicating that the current bit is correct . It sends a 0 when a bad bit is noted (1 percent of the time). The entropy or information rate of the bit minder source is $-(0.99 \log_2 0.99 + 0.01 \log_2 0.01) = 0.081$ bits per symbol. The entropy of the bit minder source is equal to equivocation.

This concept, combined with an understanding of the impact of noise on the channel, in terms of $H_y(x)$, leads to an important theorem in correcting errors.

If the correction channel has a capacity $H_y(x)$, it is possible to encode the correction data so as to send it over this channel and correct all but an arbitrarily small fraction ε of the errors. This is not possible if the channel capacity is less than $H_y(x)$.

In a real-world communications system, you do not have the luxury of a separate correction channel. Any channel capacity that is devoted to the correction channel must be subtracted from the primary information channel. The capacity of a noisy channel should still be the maximum possible of transmission. This is achieved by matching the source to the channel. In the presence of noise, the channel capacity is defined as follows.

For a source with entropy $H(x)$ and a channel with equivocation characterized by $H_y(x)$, the channel capacity is

$$C = \text{Max } [H(x) - H_y(x)]$$

where the maximum is with respect to all possible information sources used as input to the channel.

Because of the properties of the entropy function, $H(x) - H_y(x) = H(y) - H_x(y)$, allowing for an alternate expression of the channel capacity. This definition says that you can determine a definite channel capacity even though you can never send information over the channel with total certainty. This result is not completely intuitive. What is clear is that by sending the information in a redundant manner, the probability of errors can be reduced. If the message is repeated many times and then compared statistically at the receiving end, the probability of errors can be made very small.

Again, intuitively, you may feel that if the transmitted message becomes redundant enough to allow correction of most of the errors, the actual transmission rate approaches zero. If this were true, there would be no well-defined channel capacity, only a capacity for a given frequency of errors with the capacity going down as permissible number of errors goes down.

The fact that the channel capacity is defined as stated is a very significant point. It states that it is possible to send information at a rate C with the frequency of errors or equivocation as small as desired by proper encoding. It is not possible, however, to send information at any rate higher than C.

To examine this further, consider the graph shown in Figure 3-3. The source entropy, $H(x)$, is plotted along the horizontal axis. The equivocation, $H_y(x)$, is plotted along the vertical axis. The point C is the channel capacity. The region above the curve is the equivocation possible for a given $H(x)$. Those points below the line cannot be obtained. In general, the points on the line also are not obtainable.

Consider the binary channel shown in Figure 3-4. This channel sends either a 0 or a 1 with probabilities P and Q, respectively. The probability that an

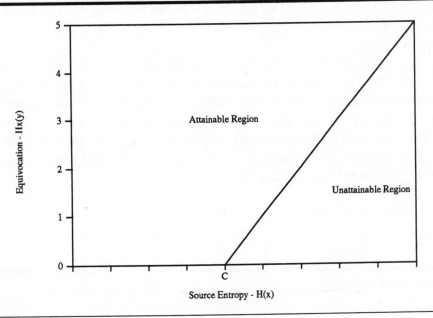

FIGURE 3-3 Possible equivocation for a given source entropy.

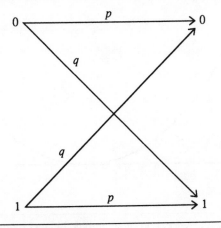

FIGURE 3-4 Symmetric binary channel.

individual signal is received correctly is p. The probability that it is wrong is $(1 - p) = q$. This channel is often referred as a *symmetric binary channel*.

The entropy of the source, $H(x)$, is $-[Q \log_2 Q + P \log_2 P]$. This entropy is maximized at a value of 1 if $P = Q = 1/2$. The equivocation, $H_y(x)$, is $-[q \log_2 q + p \log_2 p]$. The channel capacity is Max $[H(x) - H_y(x)]$. The values of p and q are functions of the channel. If $p = 1$, $H_y(x) = 0$ and the channel is essentially noiseless. If $p = 1/2$, $H_y(x) = 1$ and the channel is capable of passing no information. The curve shown in Figure 3-5 shows the capacity of the channel for all possible values of p. Notice that the curve is symmetric about $p = 1/2$. This demonstrates the fact that a channel that is usually wrong is just as good as one that is usually right.

This result can be generalized somewhat. If each input symbol has the same set of transition probabilities and the same is true of each output symbol, $H_x(y)$ is independent of the distribution probabilities on the input symbols and is equal to the $-\sum p_i \log_2 p_i$. The maximum channel capacity becomes Max $H(y) + \sum p_i \log_2 p_i$. The maximum of $H(y)$ is clearly $\log_2 m$, where m is the number of output symbols. They are made equally likely by making all the input symbols equally likely. The channel capacity then becomes

$$C = \log_2 m + \sum p_i \log_2 p_i$$

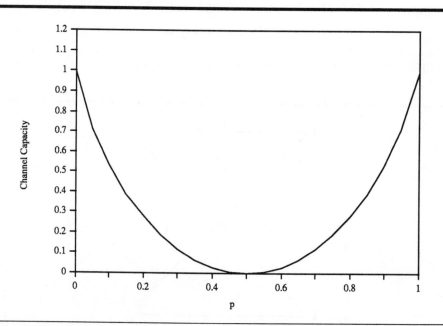

FIGURE 3-5   Channel capacity for a noisy symmetric binary channel.

These results lead to the fundamental theorem for a discrete channel with noise. The theorem is as follows.

> Let a discrete channel have the capacity C and a discrete source the entropy H per second. If $H \leq C$, there exists a coding system such that the output of the source can be transmitted over the channel with an arbitrarily small frequency of errors. If $H > C$, it is possible to encode the source so the equivocation is less than $H - C + \varepsilon$ where ε is arbitrarily small. There is no method of encoding that gives an equivocation less than $H - C$.

Consider a system that sends two channel symbols (0 and 1) over a channel. The channel is such that noise affects the symbols in groups of seven. A block of seven symbols either is transmitted correctly or exactly one of the seven symbols is incorrect. The eight possibilities (all symbols correct or one of seven is incorrect) are equally likely. Although this system is somewhat contrived, it does allow the demonstration of an efficient code. The channel capacity is

$$
\begin{aligned}
C &= \text{Max } [H(y) - H_x(y)] \\
&= 1/7[7 + 8/8 \log_2 1/8] \\
&= 4/7 \text{ bits per symbol}
\end{aligned}
$$

An efficient coding scheme, called *Hamming coding,* allows the complete detection and correction of all errors in this system. (The Hamming code will be discussed in detail later in the chapter. It is used here without discussion for demonstration of an efficient coding scheme.) The scheme is as follows. Each block consists of seven symbols, $X_1, X_2, \ldots, X_7$. Of these, X_3, X_5, X_6, and X_7 are the message symbols. X_1, X_2, and X_4 are redundant symbols. They are calculated as follows:

X_4 is chosen to make $\alpha = X_4 + X_5 + X_6 + X_7$ even
X_2 is chosen to make $\beta = X_2 + X_3 + X_6 + X_7$ even
X_1 is chosen to make $\gamma = X_1 + X_3 + X_5 + X_7$ even

When a block of seven symbols is received, α, β, and γ are calculated with even sums being set to 0 and odd sums set to 1. If the value $\alpha\beta\gamma$ is zero, there is no error. Otherwise $\alpha\beta\gamma$ is the subscript of the symbol (in binary) that is in error. By using three redundant symbols, every error can be both detected and corrected. Because of the redundancy, you are sending only 4/7 bits per symbol.

This, however, is equal to the channel capacity, implying that the coding scheme is efficient.

The need to contrive a special example to exhibit an efficient coding scheme demonstrates a basic weakness in the coding theorem. This is that the theorem is not proved by exhibiting a coding method that has the desired properties. Instead, the proof shows that a code must exist within a certain group of codes. As a result, except in some trivial cases and certain limiting situations, no explicit description of an ideal coding scheme has been found. There are, however, many useful coding schemes that are applicable to different types of information transmission.

CODING

Coding is an important aspect of data communications. Because most communication is done as a stream of binary (0 or 1) bits, almost every piece of information that is passed has to be encoded before being passed over the communications channel. After it is received, it has to be decoded to convey the desired information to the receiver. The process of encoding text or series of numbers into binary strings is a common practice. The computer uses distinct binary patterns to send letters from a keyboard to the computer and from the computer to the monitor. Much of the text stored in computer files utilizes the ASCII format, which uses 7 or 8 bits to store each letter.

The previous section showed that coding has two important aspects that are affected by the information content of the message. First, proper encoding of the original source can remove some of its inherent redundancy. The compressed information can be transmitted with fewer bits, thereby better utilizing the available channel capacity. Compressed information also requires less storage than that of its original form. Second, proper encoding can make it possible to detect and even correct errors that occur as the signal passes over the communication channel. This detection and correction can be done at the receiving end with no further information from the source.

In some respects, these two concepts are in conflict. One tries to reduce redundancy while the other increases it. Indeed, this is a basic tenet of data communications. You can have it right or you can have it fast, but you cannot have it right and fast. This may be a slight overstatement of the conflict, but it is true. The transmission rate and error correction capability must be considered in combination with the characteristics of the data channel to arrive at the optimum system.

Coding has one more important aspect, that of privacy. As digital communication becomes more and more common and more and more information is passed over channels that can be intercepted without the knowledge of either the sender or receiver, it becomes increasingly important to use some type of coding that limits the number of people who, if they receive the message, can decipher it.

Maximum Entropy Coding

In the early days of telegraphy, an enterprising young man realized that a significant number of the messages he was sending every day were very similar. Messages like "Happy Birthday" and "Congratulations to the bride and groom" seemed to appear over and over. To save himself some work and to make more money for the telegraph company, he devised a code book of standard messages with unique numbers for each message. Now, instead of sending "Melissa, Happy Birthday, George," he could send "Melissa, MX01, George," where MX01 was the unique number for "Happy Birthday." By making the message MX0102, George could add "Hugs and kisses" to his telegram.

The concept of encoding messages into a distinct set of symbols is still in wide use today. Examples regularly appear in the newspaper in the classified ads and baseball box scores. The stock market ticker is a steady stream of symbols conveying a great deal of information.

The technique is very important to data communications as well. If you assume that each transmitted symbol requires the same amount of time to send over the communication channel, the transmission time for a message is directly proportional to the number of symbols required to send it. Because transmission time is one of the major cost factors in communication, it is always advantageous to reduce the number of symbols per message.

The concept of information entropy provides a useful measure for determining how many symbols are needed to transmit a set of messages and how efficient the sequence of symbols are. If the symbols being generated from a source are all equally likely, the source has the maximum entropy value for the number of symbols. Developing a coding scheme for such a source that makes full efficient use of the available channel is straightforward as long as you can send the same number of distinct symbols over the channel.

In the real world of data communications, there are two obstacles that prevent this simple solution. First, the channel is generally limited to only two symbols, 0 and 1. Second, the symbols emanating from the source rarely occur with equal probabilities.

In the example shown earlier, you saw how an appropriate coding scheme enables the source symbols to be encoded in such a manner that the channel utilization is 100 percent. What this coding scheme did is make the channel symbols, 0 and 1, equally likely in the stream of bits that was passed over the communication channel. As noted in the example, the encoding scheme used is called *Huffman coding* after David Huffman, who first proposed the scheme.

Consider a communication channel that used D different symbols to encode a sequence of messages. For simplicity, assume that the D symbols can be represented as integer numbers, 0, 1, 2, . . . , $D - 1$. In general D can be any number, but it is usually 2, meaning the channel symbols are 0 and 1.

Let N be the number of different messages that will be sent over the channel. Each message has a probability associated with, p_i. The length of a message, L_i, is defined as the number of channel symbols required to encode the ith message. Therefore, the average message length is $L_{av} = \sum p_i L_i$.

Now assume that the source is capable of sending messages or information as fast as the channel can transmit them. In other words, the limiting link in the rate of information transfer is the channel capacity, the number of channel symbols the channel can pass in a given time period. In this situation, the coding scheme, or *ensemble code*, which results in the minimum value for L_{av} is defined as the *maximum entropy code*. Alternately, it can be called the *minimum redundancy code* or the *optimum code*. The formal definition is as follows.

The *maximum entropy* code is an ensemble code which, for a message ensemble consisting of a finite number of members, N, and for a given number of coding digits, D, yields the lowest possible average message length.

To make the coding scheme useful, two additional requirements are placed on it:

1. No two messages will consist of identical arrangements of coding digits.
2. The message codes will be constructed in such a way that no additional information is necessary to specify where a message code begins and ends once the starting point of the sequence of messages is known.

These two requirements ensure that the maximum entropy coding scheme is uniquely decodeable. The second restriction is particularly important and not quite as obvious as the first requirement. It requires that no message be coded in such a way that its code appears, digit for digit, as the first part of any other message code of greater length. No code can be a prefix of another code.

As a bad example, consider the following coding scheme for the messages, $A, B, C,$ and D.

A	0
B	1
C	10
D	11

This sequence meets the requirement that each code be unique. But consider the sequence for *ABCABD*. Using the code, this becomes 0 1 10 0 1 11. Unfortunately, the transmitted code does not contain spaces, so the transmitted message is 01100111. This string can be decoded in several different ways, each producing a different result. Three examples are:

0 1 10 0 1 11	*ABCABD*
0 11 0 0 1 11	*ADAABD*
0 1 1 0 0 1 1 1	*ABBAABBB*

A necessary condition for minimizing the average length of the encoded messages is that the length of a given message code never be longer than the length of a more probable message code. If this condition is not met, you could exchange the two message codes and obtain a smaller average length. On the other hand, if there are messages with equal probability but different code lengths, the codes for these messages can be interchanged with no effect on the average length.

The net result of this condition is that if you order the messages by their probabilities such that

$$p_1 \geq p_2 \geq \cdots \geq p_{N-1} \geq p_N$$

the lengths of the messages in the optimum coding scheme will be in a similar order, but in decreasing magnitude, i.e.,

$$L_1 \leq L_2 \leq \cdots \leq L_{N-1} \leq L_N$$

Now consider the number of digits in the longest message, L_N. If there is only one message of length L_N, there is only one message of length $L_N - 1$, because no other message could have the same prefix. But if you changed the value of the last digit in the message of length $L_N - 1$, it would be different and could be used in place of the message of length L_N. This line of reasoning results in another condition for an optimum code, that at least two (but no more than D) messages have lengths of L_N. Furthermore, all messages of lengths L_N have identical prefixes of lengths $L_N - 1$.

There is one more requirement for an optimum code. Assume that there exists some combination of D different digits of length less than L_N, but that the combination is neither a code nor a code prefix in the coding scheme. If you substitute this combination for a message of length L_N, you will reduce the average message length. Therefore, if the code is optimum, no unused combination exists. All possible sequences of length $L_N - 1$ are either codes or code prefixes.

In summary of the previous discussion, there are three additional requirements for an optimum code. These are:

3. $L_1 \le L_2 \le \cdots \le L_{N-1} \le L_N$
4. At least two, but not more than D, of the messages with code length L_N have codes that are identical except for their final digit.
5. Each possible sequence of $L_N - 1$ digits must be used either as a message code or a message code prefix.

These five requirements suggest a methodology for developing an optimum code for a given finite set of messages. Although the method can be extended for any value of D, the case of $D = 2$ covers most practical data communications systems.

The first step is to rank the messages in order of probability from highest to lowest. From the optimum code requirements, the two messages with the lowest probability will have length L_N. The codes for these two messages will be identical except that the last digit will be 0 for one and 1 for the other.

These two least probable messages can now be thought of as a single message indicated by their prefix of length $L_N - 1$. The probability of the single composite message is the sum of the original two messages. With this composite message, you now have a new ensemble of messages that is one less than the original set. If necessary, the messages are reranked according to their probabilities. The process is then repeated until only two probabilities remain and their sum is 1.

The length of each encoded message is determined by the number of times the message is combined with other messages before completing the process. If a message is combined four times, its encoding will require four digits.

When combining probabilities, there may be times when there is more than one message or composite message with the same probability. Because it is possible to rearrange the order of messages with equal probability in determining the average length of a message, the choice of which one of equal probabilities is used is of no consequence. This procedure is always sufficient to always establish the optimum binary code.

The assigning of digits to each of the combination decisions can be somewhat arbitrary. If a total of ten combinations are used to reduce the initial message set, there are $2^{10} = 1,024$ possible ways of assigning digits. Because of the nature of the construction, each way will provide a code with no common elements that is uniquely decodeable.

The best way to see how Huffman coding works is to follow a few examples. Consider a source that consists of eight equally likely symbols, A through H, ($p_i = 1/8$). The optimum coding process is shown in Figure 3-6. The denominator of 8 is omitted from the figure.

In the figure, the symbols are ordered by their probabilities, in this case all equal. At each step, you combine the two probabilities with the lowest values to form a new event. You then reorder the probabilities and repeat the process. Continue this until the probability of the event is 1.

Because the coding takes seven steps, there are 2^7 possible arrangements of 0's and 1's. Regardless of the sequences chosen, the number of channel symbols used for each symbol is equal to three. This is as you might expect, because the source symbols are equally likely and the number of symbols is an integral

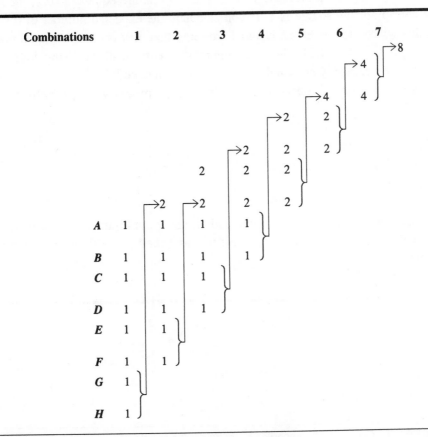

FIGURE 3-6 Optimum binary coding procedure—8 symbols.

power of 2. One of the 256 possible implementations of the code, shown in Table 3-3, is simply binary counting.

TABLE 3-3 Optimum Code—8 symbols.

Symbol	Code	p_i	L_i	p_iL_i
A	000	1/8	3	3/8
B	001	1/8	3	3/8
C	010	1/8	3	3/8
D	011	1/8	3	3/8
E	100	1/8	3	3/8
F	101	1/8	3	3/8
G	110	1/8	3	3/8
H	111	1/8	3	3/8
		Average Length		**3**

Because this example uses source symbols that are equally likely, the relative entropy of the source is 1. If you calculate the expected number of 0's and 1's that will be sent over the channel, you find that they occur with equal probability [$p(0) = p(1) = 1/2$]. Therefore, the relative entropy of the channel also is 1. If it were otherwise, you would not have an optimum code.

Now consider a source that sends three symbols with probabilities as follows:

A   1/2
B   1/3
C   1/6

The construction of the optimum code is shown in Figure 3-7. Again, at each step you add the lowest two probabilities and then place their sum as a new event.

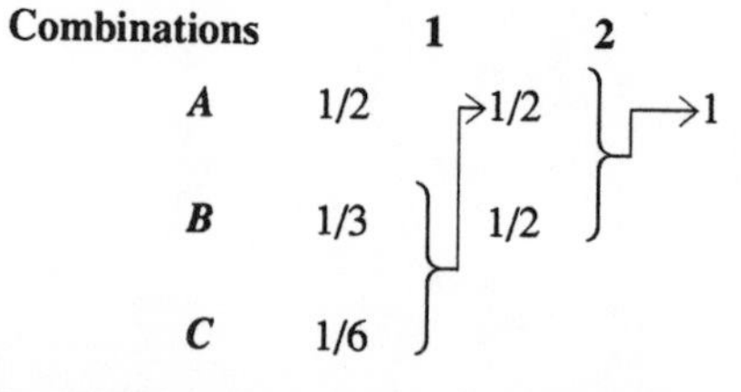

FIGURE 3-7 Optimum binary coding procedure—3 symbols.

Because there are two combinations, denoted by the brackets in the figure, there are $2^2 = 4$ possible ways of assigning digits. Each way produces the same minimum average code length of 3/2, as shown in Table 3-4.

TABLE 3-4   Optimum codes—3 symbols.

Symbol	Code 1	Code 2	Code 3	Code 4	p_i	L_i	p_iL_i
A	0	0	1	1	1/2	1	1/2
B	10	11	01	00	1/3	2	2/3
C	11	10	00	01	1/6	2	1/3
					Average Length		3/2

To demonstrate the value of the coding, compare the source entropy with the channel entropy. The source entropy is calculated on the basis of the probability of the appearance of A, B, or C. In the first case, the source entropy is 1.459 bits per symbol; relative entropy is 0.920.

The channel entropy is found by first determining the probability of occurrence of the channel symbols, 0 and 1. From code 1 of Table 3-4, the expected number of 0's is 5/6 per symbol. The expected number of 1's is 4/6 per symbol. From this $p(0) = 5/9$ and $p(1) = 4/9$. The entropy of the channel, 0.9911 bits per channel symbol, is also the relative entropy. You can see that by encoding, you are able to make better use of the channel capacity.

For a slightly more complicated code, assume that the same symbols are used with the same probabilities, but that the symbols are encoded in pairs. The coding scheme will encode two symbols at once. The symbol pairs and associated probabilities are:

AA 9/36
AB 6/36
BA 6/36
BB 4/36
AC 3/36
CA 3/36
BC 2/36
CB 2/36
CC 1/36

You can think of this as sending nine different symbols over the channel. The reduction scheme for this is a little more complicated than before, but it is still straightforward. The process is shown in Figure 3-8. For convenience, the denominator of 36 is omitted from the figure.

Because the code consists of eight combinations, there are 256 possible codes, all unique, all with the same average length. One possible code is shown in Table 3-5.

An interesting result is that it takes fewer digits on average to transmit the symbols in pairs than individually. Sending the symbols one at a time requires 1.5 digits per symbol. Sending them in pairs requires 2.972 digits per two symbols, or 1.486 digits per symbol. This result holds in general in that as there are more symbols grouped together before encoding, there are fewer digits per symbol required in the optimum code.

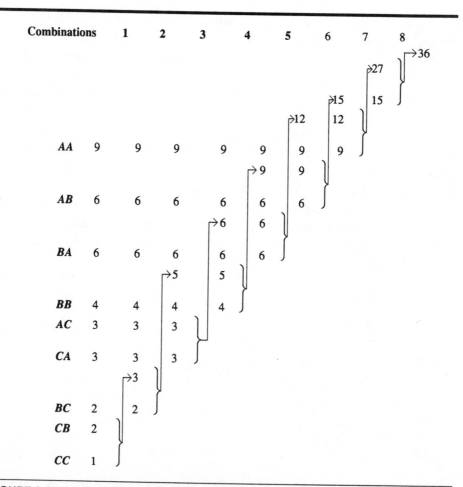

FIGURE 3-8 Optimum binary coding procedure—9 symbols.

TABLE 3-5 Optimum code—9 symbols.

Symbol	Code	p_i	L_i	$p_i L_i$
AA	00	9/36	2	18/36
AB	10	6/36	2	12/36
BA	010	6/36	3	18/36
BB	110	4/36	3	12/36
AC	0001	3/36	4	12/36
CA	1111	3/36	4	12/36
BC	1110	2/36	4	8/36
CB	01101	2/36	5	10/36
CC	01100	1/36	5	5/36
		Average Length		**107/36**

The source entropy is simply twice that of one symbol, or 2.918. The relative entropy remains at 0.920. The channel entropy, however, increases slightly because of change in the relative occurrence of the 0's and 1's. Using the code described in Table 3-5, $p(0) = 0.542$ and $p(1) = 0.458$. The relative entropy of the channel is 0.9949.

The indication is that by increasing the number of symbols that are combined into a single entity before coding, you can reduce the average number of channel digits per symbol and increase the relative entropy of the channel. Extending this premise to long strings of symbols and long code strings implies that you can make the coding as arbitrarily close to the ideal as you desire. But, as in the case of all good things, there is a catch.

The catch is that the symbols first must be encoded at the transmitter and then decoded at the receiving end. This encoding and decoding require processing time that may not always be available. At best, there is a tradeoff between the cost of processing time required to encode and decode and savings from increased channel efficiency. Also, the receiving end must know *how* the message is encoded. If the same message set with the same source symbol frequencies is sent over and over, this is not a problem. But if the message set changes continually, you have to continually change the coding scheme. You may use up channel capacity telling the receiver what the code is every time it changes.

Lempel-Ziv-Welch Algorithm

These problems are greatly reduced by using a data compression algorithm originally developed by Lempel and Ziv and then expanded by Welch. The algorithm, commonly referred to as the LZW algorithm, forms the basis for the data compressions routines in common use on many computers today. Examples are the UNIX COMPRESS utility and the many archive programs available for personal computers.

The LZW algorithm has several favorable properties.

1. It dynamically adapts to the redundancy characteristics of the specific data being compressed. No information as to the structure of the data is required before the compression operation.
2. It is implemented in a form that is transparent to a user except for a decrease in system performance.
3. The compression is "noiseless." The compressed data is an exact replica of the original.
4. The compressed information is self-decoding. It contains all the necessary information for the decompression operation.
5. The algorithm is easily implemented.

The LZW algorithm replaces strings of characters with a single code. The encoding is done without any prior analysis of the information. Instead, the process just adds every new string it sees to a table of strings that is built dynamically. Compression occurs when a single code replaces a string of characters.

In practice, the table of strings cannot expand without bound. Also, the minimum size of the code table must accommodate the complete set of symbols expected in the initial source. The use of 12-bit codes is common. Generally, the first 256 codes are used for the standard 8-bit computer codes. Then the remaining 3,840 codes (4,096 − 256) are assigned as the algorithm works its way through the source.

The compression algorithm is called a "greedy" parsing algorithm, because the input string is examined character by character in a serial fashion in one pass. The longest recognized input string is parsed off each time. A recognized string is one that exists in the string table. Strings added to the string table are determined by the parsing. Each parsed input string extended by its next input character forms a new string added to the string table. Each added string is assigned a unique identifier, namely its code value. The compression algorithm is shown in Figure 3-9.

For a simple example, consider the source from the previous section, a three-letter alphabet (A, B, and C) with probabilities of 1/2, 1/3, and 1/6, respectively. A sample stream of characters is ABAAB CBBBC BAABA ACAAA. The first step is to assign each individual a code character. For simplicity, use 1, 2, and 3 for A, B, and C respectively. The compression process is shown in Table 3-6.

A primary concern is storing the string table. The example generated 15 codes, some as long as three characters. The method generally used is to store

```
Initialize string table with single-character strings

STRING = first input character

WHILE there are still input characters DO

    CHARACTER = next input character
    IF STRING + CHARACTER is in string table, THEN
        STRING = STRING + CHARACTER
    ELSE
        output the code for STRING
        add STRING + CHARACTER to the string table
        STRING = CHARACTER
    END of IF

END of WHILE

output the code for STRING
```

FIGURE 3-9 LZW compression algorithm.

TABLE 3-6 Compression process.

STRING	CHARACTER	Output	String Table
			1 = A
			2 = B
			3 = C
A	B	1	4 = AB
B	A	2	5 = BA
A	A	1	6 = AA
A	B	...	...
AB	C	4	7 = ABC
C	B	3	8 = CB
B	B	2	9 = BB
B	B	...	...
BB	C	9	10 = BBC
C	B	...	...
CB	A	8	11 = CBA
A	A	...	...
AA	B	6	12 = AAB
B	A	...	...
BA	A	5	13 = BAA
A	A	...	...
AA	C	6	14 = AAC
C	A	3	15 = CA
A	A	...	...

the code as a combination of the prefix and the new character. From the example, code 4 becomes 1B, code 5 is 2A, code 6 is 1A, code 7 is 4C, etc. This form of storage also is conducive to hashing methods that enhance the code look-up process.

As stated earlier, one of the benefits of the LZW algorithm is that it does not require the transmission of a translation table. The decompression process reconstructs the string table as the message is decoded. Each received code is translated into a prefix string and an extension character.

The string table is updated as each code is received. When a code has been translated, its first character is used as the extension character, combined with the prior string, to add a new string to the string table. This new string is assigned a unique code value, which is the same code that was assigned in the compression process. The algorithm for the decompression process is shown in Figure 3-10.

Continuing with the example, you can use this algorithm to decompress the transmitted message, as shown in Table 3-7.

Although the example does demonstrate the process of compression and decompression, it does not exhibit a good compression ratio, because the source itself is a relatively efficient source. As showed earlier, its inherent redundancy is less than 8 percent. English text, on the other hand, has a redundancy of almost 50 percent. Also, the number of symbols in the source is not large enough to start to see the advantages gained from repeating symbol patterns. If the list of source symbols was several hundred, you would start to see good compression.

The LZW algorithm, however, is capable of providing compression ratios of 2 to 1 for text files. This agrees well with the redundancy estimate for English

```
Read OLDCODE
Output OLDCODE
WHILE there are still input characters DO
     Read NEWCODE
     IF NEWCODE is not in string table THEN
          STRING = translation of OLDCODE
          STRING = STRING + CHARACTER
     ELSE
          STRING = translation of NEWCODE
     END of IF
     output STRING
     CHARACTER = first character of string
     add OLDCODE + CHARACTER to string table
     OLDCODE = NEWCODE
END of WHILE
```

FIGURE 3-10 LZW decompression algorithm.

TABLE 3-7 Decompression process.

OLDCODE	NEWCODE	STRING	Output	CHARACTER	String Table
					1 = A
					2 = B
					3 = C
1	...	...	A	...	...
1	2	B	B	B	4 = AB
2	1	A	A	A	5 = BA
1	4	AB	AB	A	6 = AA
4	3	C	C	C	7 = ABC
3	2	B	B	B	8 = CB
2	9	B	BB	B	9 = BB
9	8	CB	CB	C	10 = BBC
8	6	AA	AA	A	11 = CBA
6	5	BA	BA	B	12 = AAB
5	6	AA	AA	A	13 = BAA
6	3	C	C	C	14 = AAC
3	6	AA	AA	A	15 = CA
6	1	A	A	A	...
2					

language text. Huffman coding, on the other hand, generally only achieves a 1.5 compression ratio for text and requires an extensive translation table. Data base files, when containing repetitive fields and large gaps for unfilled fields, can often be compressed to as small as 10 to 25 percent of their original size using the LZW algorithm.

One last note on the LZW algorithm. Welch is listed as the inventor of U.S. Patent 4,558,302, "High Speed Data Compression and Decompression Apparatus and Method," December 1985. The patent is assigned to Sperry Corporation, now UNISYS. UNISYS has not pressed its claim on the patent to date, but may at a later time. Caution must be exercised in using the LZW algorithm in a commercial product.

Error Detection/Error Correction Coding

Both Huffman coding and LZW compression work on the premise that there is either no noise on the channel or that all noise can be compensated for. Because the coding process removes most of the redundancy in the original information, any corruption of the transmitted signal is likely to go undetected. After all, if a message has no redundancy, all received messages have meaning, whether they are right or wrong. Both schemes also provide messages with lesser redundancy as the number of possible codes is increased. More codes imply more data channel symbols for each code. Because more channel symbols are required to send a single code word, the likelihood that one or more channel symbol is incorrect is higher.

An approximation to an ideal coding scheme should have the property that if the signal is altered in a reasonable way by noise, the original can still be recovered. If the coding scheme is good, the noise alteration does not bring the signal closer to another reasonable signal than the original. This goodness is accomplished at the cost of injecting an amount of redundancy into the coding. Ideally, the redundancy is tailored to combat the type of noise present on the channel.

Coding to improve error detection and to allow error correction is generally done with the channel symbols only. The error reduction coding process assumes that the source message has already been encoded to maximize its information content. The error coding process operates on a series of binary digits, 0 or 1.

Another concept used in error detection and correcting is to consider that the code is sent in blocks of n binary digits. These are defined as *systematic codes*. Each block of n digits contains m digits of information and $k = n - m$ digits that are redundant. The redundant digits can be used to detect and correct errors in both themselves and the information digits. n and m can be used to express the redundancy of the error detecting/error correcting code.

> The *redundancy R* is the ratio of the number of digits used in each block (n) to the minimum number of digits required to convey the information (m), or $R = n/m$.

This definition of redundancy is consistent with the information theory concept of redundancy. It does assume that the message information has already been encoded in such a way that its relative entropy is 1.

A geometric model is a useful analogy in the development and study of error detecting and correcting codes. The model consists of an n-dimensional cube. The code points form a subset of the set of all vertices of the hypercube.

In this space of 2^n points, a *metric D(x, y)* is defined as a distance between two points x and y. $D(x, y)$ is further defined as equal to the number of coordinates in x and y that are different. In a geometric sense, it is equal to the number of edges you must travel along to go from x to y. The function satisfies the three conditions of a metric:

$D(x, y) = 0$ if and on if $x = y$
$D(x, y) = D(y, x) > 0$ for all $x \neq y$
$D(x, y) + D(y, z) \geq D(x, z)$

If all codes are unique, $D(x, y) \geq 1$ for all $x \neq y$. For example, let $n = 3$. There are eight possible codes:

000   001   010   011   100   101   110   111

If any one of these codes is sent over a channel and a single error occurs, the code becomes another value. Although the codes are unique, they also possess the property that all single errors are interpreted as a wrong code. This does not meet the criteria described earlier for an ideal coding scheme. The corruption of a single digit not only brings the code value closer to another acceptable code, it actually transforms the code value into another acceptable value.

Another way to look at this is to examine the number of digits that contain information and the number that are redundant. In this case, all digits possess information. No digits are redundant. This implies that $n = 3$, $m = 3$, and $R = 3/3 = 1$.

If you want $D(x, y) \geq 2$, there are now two sets of four possible codes:

000   010   100   110

or

001   011   101   111

In this case, two digits contain information and one is redundant, implying that $R = 3/2$. If any one of these codes is sent over a channel and a single error occurs, the received code corresponds to no acceptable code value. When you try to interpret the code, you cannot find an acceptable value. Therefore you know that an error occurred as the code passed over the communication channel. This implies that if the coding is such that $D(x, y) \geq 2$, all single digit errors can be detected.

Although you know an error occurred, you cannot make an intelligent choice as to what the correct value is. The erroneous code, although it is known to be bad, is spaced equidistant from two acceptable codes. To determine which code is correct, you might as well flip a coin.

If, on the other hand, the code is such that $D(x, y) \geq 3$, movement away from an acceptable code by a single error still leaves it closer to that code than to any other code. This implies that if $D(x, y) \geq 3$, all single digit errors can be both detected and corrected. With $n = 3$, there are four sets of two possible codes:

000	and	111
001	and	110
010	and	101
011	and	100

These codes are equivalent, so examine the first combination, 000 and 111. What it amounts to is repeating every source binary digit three times as it is sent over the communication channel. At the receiving end, if you assume that the original source digit is the value that makes up the majority of a three-digit block of received digits, you can now indeed detect and correct all single digit errors. As you may notice, this code is redundant, sending three digits for every digit of information. The redundancy R has now grown to 3.

If you want a code that meets the condition $D(x, y) \geq 4$, you end up with eight sets of single codes. In effect, you are sending the same code all the time. If you ever fail to receive the code, you know both that it is wrong and that it should be the original code. Unfortunately, you are not passing any information over the channel.

Now consider what happens if two errors occur in one block. In the case of $D \geq 1$, you are no worse off than before. You still have no idea that errors have occurred, because the received information conforms with acceptable code values. This same behavior now also exists when $D \geq 2$. Two errors in a block move one code value to another acceptable code value. When two errors occur, a code with $D \geq 2$ is not better than one with $D \geq 1$.

If $D \geq 3$, two errors will result in a code that is not an allowable value. The two errors also move the code closer to the wrong value than to the right value. If you knew that the errors only occurred in pairs, you could assume that the correct code when an error is detected is the one farthest from the received value. In general, you do not know if one or two errors occurred. You can detect single or double errors, but you are back to flipping a coin to correct it.

To generalize these results, return to the geometric model. An ideal code for a given D has its valid code points located such that the minimum distance from any code point to any other code point is $\geq D$. You can think of each code point lying at the center of a sphere with a radius of D. The other code points are located at points defined by the intersection of the surfaces of the sphere around each valid code point.

The minimum value of D for a given set of code points is important to the capability of the code to detect and correct errors. D is often referred to as the

Hamming distance. If $D \geq 1$, the code values are unique, but they have no error detection or correction capability. If $D \geq 2$, single errors in a given block result in meaningless symbols, therefore they are detectable. If $D \geq 3$, single errors leave the decoded value still closer to the correct value than any other. In this case, single errors are both detectable and correctable. These results are summarized in Table 3-8.

TABLE 3-8 Hamming distances.

Minimum Distance	Meaning
1	Uniqueness
2	Single error detection
3	Single error correction
4	Single error correction plus double error detection
5	Double error correction
	etc.

For a specified minimum distance, detection and correction are interchangeable. For example, for $D \geq 5$, you can achieve double error detection and correction, single error detection and correction plus triple error detection, or quadruple error detection.

The class of codes that conform to the minimum D constraints are called *Hamming codes.* While the value of D tells you how well a code will do in terms of error correction and detection, it does not tell you how to construct the code. Nor does it tell you how to actually correct an error after it is detected. For the lower values of D, it is possible to develop coding schemes that are relatively easy to implement.

The simplest case is $D \geq 2$, single error detection. Single error detection is essentially parity checking, a procedure embedded in most computer processes such as memory transfers, disk accesses, etc. If the given block length is n, let the first $n - 1$ positions contain $n - 1$ digits of information. The nth is the parity position. It is set to 0 or 1 so that the sum of the zeroes or ones in the first $n - 1$ positions is even (or odd). This is called even parity (or odd parity). On the receiving end, the sum of $n - 1$ digits are compared with the parity digit. If they do not agree, a single error has occurred.

Parity checking actually detects all odd numbers of errors, because an odd number of moves from an acceptable value will always result in an unacceptable value. If the number of errors is even, the errors are not detected.

The redundancy of the parity checking scheme is easily calculated because $m = n - 1$,

$$R = n / (n - 1) = 1 + 1 / (n - 1)$$

From this expression, you might feel that you can move the redundancy of the code arbitrarily close to unity by increasing n, the number of digits in each block. This is true, but at the cost of increasing the probability of a single detectable error and an undetectable double error. If you assume that $p \ll 1$ is the probability of an error in any single digit, then for n as large as $1/p$, the probability of having a correct symbol (no errors) is $1/e = 0.3679$. The probability of a double error is $1/2e = 0.1839$.

The concept of parity checking also can be applied over groups of digits within a code block. This technique is used to implement single error correcting codes.

Consider a code consisting of n digits, with m digits containing information and $k = n - m$ being parity digits. When you receive a code symbol, you apply k parity checks. The results of the parity checks are denoted by a 0 (implying that the check is valid) or a 1 (implying an error in the digits that were checked). The results can be combined in a string of k digits to form the *checking number*.

The checking number must describe $m + k + 1 = n + 1$ possible things (an error in one and only one of the n digits or all digits correct). Therefore

$$2^k \geq m + k + 1 \quad \text{or} \quad 2^m \leq 2^n / (n + 1)$$

This condition for n, m, and k can be used to construct Table 3-9, which shows the necessary values of m and k to detect and correct single errors in codes of n digits.

Now that the number of check bits is known, you have to decide where they will be located. In theory the check bits can be located anywhere within the block. By proper placement, however, the check digits, when combined to form a single value, will indicate the location of the digit where the error occurred.

The first digit indicates if an error occurred in any location whose location number has a 1 as its rightmost digit (binary representation). This is all odd positions, i.e., 1, 3, 5, ... For simplicity, the check digit itself is placed in position 1. Its value is dependent on the values in positions 3, 5, 7, ...

The second check digit indicates if an error occurred in any location having a 1 in the position second from the right. These positions are 2, 3, 6, 7, 10, 11, ... Again, the check digit itself is located in position 2. A similar criteria is followed as additional check digits are added. Table 3-10 summarizes the results.

TABLE 3-9 Single error correction n, m, and k.

n	m	k
1	0	1
2	0	2
3	1	2
4	1	3
5	2	3
6	3	3
7	4	3
8	4	4
9	5	4
10	6	4
11	7	4
12	8	4
13	9	4
14	10	4
15	11	4
16	11	5
	Etc.	

TABLE 3-10 Check digits for single error correction.

Check Number	Check Position	Positions Checked
1	1	1, 3, 5, 7, 9, 11, 13, 15, 17, ...
2	2	2, 3, 6, 7, 10, 11, 14, 15, 18, ...
3	4	4, 5, 6, 7, 12, 13, 14, 15, 20, ...
4	8	8, 9, 10, 11, 12, 13, 14, 15, 24, ...
.	.	.
.	.	.
.	.	.

From Table 3-9, for $n = 7$, $m = 4$ and $k = 3$. From Table 3-10, the check digits are located in positions 1, 2, and 4. Positions 3, 5, 6, and 7 contain the message information. The result is $2^4 = 16$ possible messages. There are $2^7 - 16 = 112$ useless messages. Check digit 1 is based on the values in positions 3, 5, and 7. Check digit 2 is based on the values in positions 3, 4, 6, and 7. Check digit 3 is based on the values in positions 4, 5, 6, and 7. The resulting possible codes, assuming even parity is used in the check positions, are shown in Table 3-11. The check digits are shown in *italics*.

TABLE 3-11   Acceptable codes for single error correction, $n = 7$.

Code Number	1	2	3	4	5	6	7
0	0	0	0	0	0	0	0
1	1	1	0	1	0	0	1
2	0	1	0	1	0	1	0
3	1	0	0	0	0	1	1
4	1	0	0	1	1	0	0
5	0	1	0	0	1	0	0
6	1	1	0	0	1	1	0
7	0	0	0	1	1	1	1
8	1	1	1	0	0	0	0
9	0	0	1	1	0	0	1
10	1	0	1	1	0	1	0
11	0	1	1	0	0	1	1
12	0	1	1	1	1	0	0
13	1	0	1	0	1	0	1
14	0	0	1	0	1	1	0
15	1	1	1	1	1	1	1

As noted earlier, determining the number of digits that make up the code block is a tradeoff between redundancy and acceptable errors levels. The redundancy of the code decreases as the number of digits increases. But as the number of digits increase, the probability of having more than one error increases.

Figure 3-11 shows the redundancy of codes that are single error detecting or single error correcting. This behavior demonstrates two points. First, as n gets large, the redundancy of both coding schemes gets arbitrarily close to unity, which is keeping the errors in control. Second, the redundancy of single error correcting codes has local minimums at values of $n = 2^k - 1$, i.e., 3, 7, 15, 31, etc.

Assume a system that uses n binary digits per block, that allows only single errors to occur in each block, and that the errors are independent. This system is, in effect, a system using the Hamming coding scheme. In the system, all channel errors are corrected by the redundant codes. The channel capacity for the system is

$$C = \text{Max } [H(y) - H_x(y)]$$
$$= 1/n[n - \log_2 (n + 1)]$$
$$= 1 - [\log_2 (n + 1)]/n \text{ bits per symbol}$$

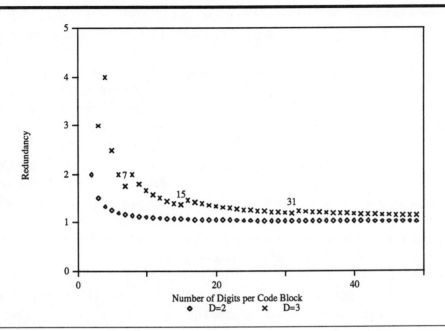

FIGURE 3-11 Hamming code redundancy.

The values of n when the Hamming code produces a local minimum in the redundancy value ($n = 3, 7, 15, 31, \ldots$) coincide with those places in which the redundancy is equal to the inverse of the channel capacity. For other values of n, the coding scheme is not as efficient. For this reason, the Hamming codes are generally implemented with $n = 3, 7, 15, 31, \ldots$.

Assume that the probability that any single digit is corrupted by noise is equal to p and that all digits are independent of each other. Now consider a block of n digits. What is the probability that no more than one error occurs in the n digits?

This is a Bernoulli trial with n attempts and probability $(1 - p)$ of success (no error). The probability that no errors occur is $(1 - p)^n$. The probability that one error occurs is $n(1 - p)^{(n-1)}p$. The probability that more than one error occurs is $1 - [(1 - p)^n + n(1 - p)^{(n-1)}p]$. This value is the probability that an undetected error occurs during the transmission of a single block.

As an example, let $n = 7$ and $p = 0.01$. The probability that no errors occur during a single block is 0.9320. The probability that one error occurs, which is assumed to be detected and corrected, is 0.0659. The probability that more than one error occurs is $1 - (0.9320 + 0.0659) = 0.0021$. In effect, you now have a system in which the probability of an undetected error in a group of seven binary digits is 0.0021. Figure 3-12 shows the probability that an undetectable error occurs when using single digit error correcting coding for code lengths of 3, 7, 15, and 31. Notice that as the length of the block increases, the probability of an undetected error also increases.

It is possible to add a single, overall parity digit to a single error correction code and achieve both single error correction and double error detection. Except for this case, the development of efficient codes for double error detection and triple error detection and even higher orders of error correction is much more difficult.

One exception noted early in the development of codes is the group of codes called *Golay codes*, after Marcel Golay. Golay attempted to extend Shannon's concept of lossless binary coding with seven symbols and only one error per block. He noted that a necessary but not sufficient condition for a lossless coding scheme in a binary system is the existence of three or more first numbers of a line of a Pascal's triangle that adds up to an exact power of 2.

Golay found that the sum of the first four terms of the 23rd line are equal to 2^{11}. This implies that a coding scheme in which $n = 23$, $m = 11$, and $k = 12$ can detect and correct three errors per block. The redundancy of this code is high, 2.091, but the error correction performance is impressive. Figure 3-13 contrasts the probability of an uncorrected error with Golay coding versus the Hamming coding for single digit error correction. The penalty paid for using Golay coding

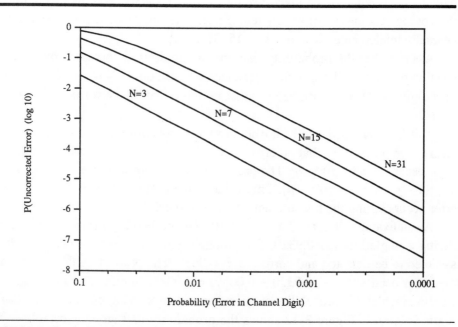

FIGURE 3-12   Probability of an undetectable error.

is the increased redundancy plus a substantial processing load to encode and decode the code blocks.

The problem with the Golay code is determining where the error occurred. In the case of the Hamming code, the location of the single error is explicitly given by the value of the parity bits. This is not the case for the Golay code. The only way to find the correct information was via an exhaustive search of all possible results. The search looked for the correct code that was closest to the received code.

The concept of algebraic coding, introduced in the early 1960s, provided a way to overcome this large processing burden associated with decoding. Algebraic coding is based on the mathematics of finite fields or *Galois fields*. A finite field contains a finite number of elements for which the operations of addition and multiplication hold, as well as the associative and commutative properties of multiplication and addition. An example of a finite field is the set of integers less than a prime number p, operating with modular p arithmetic. Binary arithmetic, numbers composed of only 0's and 1's, forms a finite field. The field GF[16] is the inclusive set of four-digit binary numbers.

If the coded block of symbols is constructed by associating each digit with an element in a Galois field, it is possible to derive an algebraic equation whose roots represent the location of the channel errors. For correction of higher

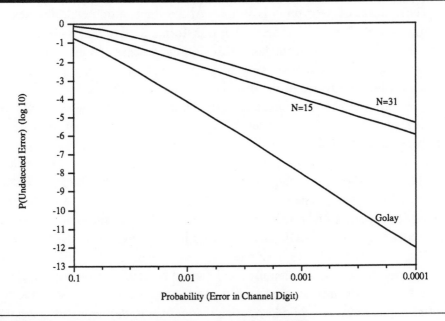

FIGURE 3-13   Probability of an undetected error (Golay code).

numbers of errors, the computations associated with finding the roots are at least an order of magnitude less than the exhaustive search required previously.

The set of codes based on using this process are called Bose-Chaudhuri-Hocquenghen (BCH) codes after their discoverers. Using BCH techniques, it is possible to correct an arbitrary number of errors occurring in a finite number of message bits. The Hamming codes for detecting and correcting single digit errors can be shown to be a BCH code for correcting a single error. The Golay code is also a BCH code.

Privacy Coding

A third reason for coding information is to ensure its privacy or authenticity. Privacy is preventing anyone but the designated addressee from using the information. Authenticity is verifying that the message sender is indeed who he says he is. As the value and volume of data that passes over communications networks has grown, there has been an increased need for communications systems that are private and tamper resistant.

Historically, the encoding of messages to ensure privacy has been limited to military or high-level government communications. Advances in electronic processing and public key encryption systems have made encryption manageable and feasible for the commercial sector. The volume and value of the data make it necessary. Privacy coding should be considered when sensitive information is passed over communication links subject to eavesdropping and interception.

The concept of encryption is simple. At the transmitting end, the message undergoes a mathematical process that transforms the original message into a form that is seemingly meaningless. Although the process may be general, there is a *key* that makes the process very specific for the transmitting source. At the receiving end, the inverse of the original mathematical operation is performed, using the specific key, to produce the original message. The mathematical process is such that without knowledge of the proper key, it is computationally infeasible to deduce.

A major difficulty in encryption systems is managing the keys. This includes distributing the keys, updating the keys, and ensuring their security. Classical cryptography techniques depend on each node in a communications net having a unique key for every other node with which it wants to communicate. A network of n nodes requires $n(n-1)/2$ keys. In order not to compromise the system, the keys have to be distributed over a completely private channel. In more traditional systems, the keys are literally hand-carried by courier to each node.

In recent years, this classical problem has been greatly alleviated by the concept of public keys. A public key is one that can be transmitted over unsecured channels. Each public key actually consists of two parts, the public part and the private part. While these two keys are obviously related (the public key is the inverse of the private key and vice versa), the relationship between the two keys is infeasible to compute, allowing one key to be made public while the other is kept secret.

Each user generates a pair of keys. Only the public key is communicated to other users. Being public information, the key can be sent over an insecure channel. It could even be published in what amounts to a key phone book.

If a plaintext P is acted on with the receiver's public key, i.e., $C = PK_R(P)$, anyone can encipher messages and send them. Only the intended receiver, however, can decipher the message.

This system also can provide authentication, the assurance that the message sender is indeed who he says he is. In this case, the sender uses his secret key to encrypt the plaintext, $C = PK_T(P)$. This is essentially a digital signature. Only the transmitter can encrypt and send these messages, but anyone can receive them and decrypt them (as long as they know the transmitter's public key). By using the transmitter's public key to decrypt the message, they verify that the message did come from the sender.

Diffie and Hellman developed a public key system based on exponentiation in $GF(p)$. A basic conjecture is that the exponentiation in $GF(p)$ is a one-way function for a large prime number p. Given an X and α, it is easy to compute the equation $Y = \alpha^X \bmod p$. But given α and Y, it is hard to compute X.

Each user generates an independent random number X_i chosen uniformly from the set of integers $\{1, 2, \ldots, p - 1\}$. The X_i is kept secret, but $Y_i = \alpha^{X_i} \bmod p$ is placed in a public file. When user i and j wish to communicate privately, they use $K_{ij} = \alpha^{X_i X_j} \bmod p$ as their key. User i obtains K_{ij} by obtaining Y_j from the public file and letting $K_{ij} = Y_j^{X_i} \bmod p$. User j obtains K_{ij} in a similar manner.

After the keys are exchanged, many different encryption systems can be used to actually encode (and then decode) the systems. The National Data Encryption Standard (DES) was published by the National Bureau of Standards (now the National Institute of Science and Technology) in 1976. It is used widely in the banking industry to secure and authenticate electronic funds transfer. Although the DES can be implemented in software, it is generally implemented via custom integrated circuits.

SUMMARY

Information theory is concerned with the mathematical laws that govern the transmission and processing of information. It deals with the measurement of information, the representation of information, and the capacity of communications systems to transmit and process information.

The entropy of a set of probabilities $p_1, p_2, \ldots, p_n$ is H where H is defined as $H = - \sum p_i \log p_i$. H is equal to 0 if and only if one probability in the process has a value of unity and all other probabilities are zero. If the number of possible events in the process is n, then the maximum value of H occurs when all events are equally likely with a probability of $1/n$. This maximum entropy value is $n\,(1/n \log_2 n) = \log_2 n$.

The ratio of entropy of a source to maximum possible entropy is the *relative entropy*. The *redundancy of a source* is 1 – relative entropy.

For source with entropy H (bits per symbol) and a channel C (bits per second), it is possible to encode the output of the source in such a way as to transmit at the average rate of $C/H - \varepsilon$ symbols per second over the channel, where ε is arbitrarily small. It is not possible to transmit at an average rate greater than C/H.

For a source with entropy $H(x)$ and a channel with equivocation characterized by $H_y(x)$, the channel capacity is $C = \text{Max}\,[H(x) - H_y(x)]$, where the maximum is with respect to all possible information sources used as input to the channel.

Coding is an important aspect of data communications. Proper encoding of the original source can remove some of its inherent redundancy. Proper encoding also can make it possible to detect and even correct errors that occur as the signal passes over the communication channel. Coding can also be used to provide data privacy and authentication.

The *maximum entropy* code is an ensemble code which, for a message ensemble consisting of a finite number of members, N, and for a given number of coding digits, D, yields the lowest possible average message length. Huffman coding provides a universal algorithm for encoding a fixed set of symbols into a binary code that is the maximum entropy code.

The Lempel-Ziv-Welch data compression algorithm provides a dynamic data compression with no requirements for prior knowledge of the original data set. The compressed information is an exact replica of the original and contains all the necessary information for the decompression operation.

An approximation to an ideal coding scheme has the property that if the signal is altered in a reasonable way by noise, the original can still be recovered. If the coding scheme is good, the noise alteration does not bring the signal closer to another reasonable signal than the original. This goodness is accomplished at the cost of injecting an amount of redundancy into the coding. Coding to improve error detection and to allow error correction is generally done with the channel symbols only. The error reduction coding process assumes that the source message has already been encoded to maximize its information content. The error coding process operates on a series of binary digits, 0 or 1.

Error detection and correcting often divides the signal into blocks of n binary digits. These are *systematic codes*. Each block of n digits contains m digits of information and $k = n - m$ digits that are redundant.

The Hamming distance, D, is a metric that determines the capacity of a code to detect and correct errors in the received signal. If $D \geq 1$, the code values are unique, but they have no error detection or correction capability. If $D \geq 2$, single errors in a given block result in meaningless symbols, and therefore are detectable. If $D \geq 3$, single errors leave the decoded value still closer to the correct value than any other. In this case, single errors are both detectable and correctable. Higher values of D provide detection and correction of multiple errors.

SUGGESTED READING

In 1948, Shannon published "The Mathematical Theory of Communication." Appearing in two successive issues of the *Bell Systems Technical Journal,* Shannon laid out in only 24 pages the basic foundations and concepts for data communications. Combining real-life examples with mathematical models, he developed theorems that possess power, elegance, and generality.

Huffman's "A Method for the Construction of Minimum Redundancy Codes" serves a similar function for the design of minimum redundancy codes. Many of the basic terms, definitions, and concepts for error detection and correction were set by Richard Hamming in his 1950 classic paper, entitled, appropriately enough, "Error Detecting and Error Correcting Codes."

These papers and others are collected in two reprint volumes, *Key Papers in the Development of Information Theory*, edited by David Slepian, and *Key Papers in the Development of Coding Theory*, edited by E. R. Berlekamp. The latter book also contains an excellent summary of the key developments of BCH coding. Berlekamp also has two other books on the subject of coding, *Error Correcting Codes* and *Algebraic Coding Theory.*

Diffie and Hellman have written numerous papers that discuss the nature of public key cryptography systems, how they are designed, and how they are implemented. The National Data Encryption Standard is described in FIPS Publication 46, published by the National Bureau of Standards in 1977.

4

GRAPH THEORY AND NETWORK FLOWS

Messages are generally passed over data communications networks via *datagrams* or *virtual circuits*. Datagrams can be thought of as letters, because they are fixed amounts of information sent from one party to another and are generally one-way communication systems. Virtual circuits are more like telephone calls. After the circuit is established, communication is generally two-way and much less structured.

Each datagram contains header information that includes its ultimate destination. As a datagram moves over a network, it is processed at a number of nodes. Each node uses the header information to determine which node to send the datagram to next. Eventually, the datagram reaches its destination and stops.

In a virtual circuit, the link between the sender and receiver is established before any information is exchanged. Once the link is established, the information exchange can continue indefinitely. A virtual circuit is ideally suited to interactive computer sessions.

Efficient communication with both datagrams and virtual circuits depends on being able to determine the optimum link between the sender and the receiver. The criteria used to determine the optimum link can include the lowest cost, the most reliable, or the fastest transmission (often the shortest path). Many of the mathematical techniques used to determine the optimum link are based on graph theory. Graph theory also provides techniques for determining the optimum number and configuration of links to provide reliable service to a distributed network of users.

In its simplest form a network consists of a series of points connected by a series of lines. The points are generally referred to as nodes, and the lines are arcs. This results in the common arc-node representation of a network, shown in Figure 4-1. The study of networks in mathematics is devoted to finding the attributes that satisfy certain conditions, using the properties of the arcs and their arrangement as they connect the nodes.

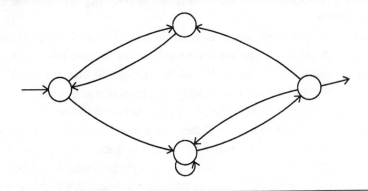

FIGURE 4-1 Arc-node network representation.

Graph theory focuses more on the properties of the arcs. Two primary properties generally associated with each arc are its length and its carrying capacity. In data communication systems, the carrying capacity is generally represented by the bandwidth of the arc or the number of bits that can be transmitted per second. Nodes generally represent processors. The properties of the processors are better treated in queueing theory, discussed in the next chapter.

FUNDAMENTALS

In graph theory, a graph $G(N, A)$ is defined as a set of points N and a set A of ordered pairs of these points. The members of N are called *nodes,* and N is called the *node set.* The members of A are called *arcs* with A called the *arc set.* In those cases in which the order of the two nodes that make up an arc is important, the arc is a *directed arc.* The arc (i, j) is a link from node i to node j. In this case i has various names, including the *start node* or *tail node.* The names for j include *end node, finish node,* and *head node.* A graph made up of directed arcs is called a *directed graph* or a *digraph.*

The graph $G(N, A)$ is often depicted with the nodes shown as small circles and the arcs shown as lines connecting the nodes. The direction of the arc is indicated with an arrow. If two nodes are connected by two directed arcs (i, j) and (j, i), the two arcs can be shown as two lines with arrows pointing in opposite directions or as a single line with no arrow.

Consider a graph consisting of four nodes, $\{1, 2, 3, 4\}$, and six arcs, $\{(1, 2), (2, 1), (2, 3), (3, 1), (3, 4), (4, 1)\}$. This graph is represented in two ways in

Figure 4-2. The position of the arcs and nodes is only important to the clarity of the representation.

If all the arcs in a graph occur in pairs so that for every arc (i, j) there is an arc (j, i), the graph is an *undirected graph*. In an undirected graph, the arcs themselves are often called *edges*. The undirected graph also forms the *underlying graph* of a directed graph. The underlying graph is one in which the direction of the arcs is not important, only the connection between the nodes.

A *network* is a graph in which all the arcs possess a property or properties in addition to end nodes. The important properties in data communications include length (generally assumed to be proportional to propagation time) and carrying capacity. The graph specified by (N, A) becomes the network (N, A, P), where P is the property or properties associated with each arc. Because there may be several properties, there is no universal representation of the properties of the arcs.

In addition to the arc's individual properties, groups of arcs can have association properties. These association properties are useful in developing algorithms for analyzing a network. The most common association properties are *chain, path, cycle,* and *circuit.*

A chain between two nodes is a series of arcs that joins the nodes. The property of joining can be accomplished in either direction. If s and t are two nodes and s is joined to an intermediate node i_1, i_1 joined to i_2, and so on until there is an rth node i_r that is joined to t, there is an $r + 1$ arc chain from s to t. Notice that because a chain goes from s to t, it is not necessarily possible to move from s to t.

To move from s to t, a path must exist between s and t. A path is a chain in which the direction of the arcs are all from s to t. A path is a chain made up of *forward arcs*. Forward arcs all move in the direction from s to t. If a chain contains a *reverse arc*, it cannot be a path.

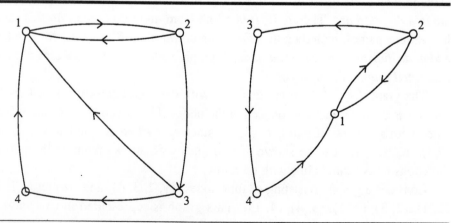

FIGURE 4-2   Simple graph representation.

A cycle is a chain whose starting node is the same as its end node. A circuit is a cycle that is also a path.

As the number of nodes and arcs in a network increase, the possible number of paths and chains can get very large, especially when cycles and circuits are allowed. *Simple paths* and *simple chains* are paths and chains that do not contain cycles.

The graph shown in Figure 4-3 demonstrates these definitions and properties. The set of arcs {(1, 3), (3, 4), (6, 4)} forms a chain between nodes 1 and 6. The chain is not a path because arc (6, 4) is a reverse arc. The set of arcs {(1, 2), (2, 5), (5, 6)} is both a chain and a path between nodes 1 and 6. It is also a simple chain and path because it contains no cycles. The arcs {(3, 1), (3, 4), (4, 5), (2, 5), (1, 2)} form a cycle that starts and ends in node 1. Because arcs (1, 3), (2, 5), and (1, 2) are reverse arcs, it is not a circuit. The arcs {(1, 2), (2, 3), (3, 1)} form a circuit.

In data communication, a path must exist from the sender to the receiver for a datagram to move from one to the other. Because transmission time is generally a function the number of nodes that the message passes through, the optimum path should not include cycles. All nodes on a circuit can be linked via a virtual circuit, because information can flow back and forth between any two nodes on the circuit.

Given a graph (N, A), you can consider other graphs that are formed by taking subsets of the nodes and arcs or of the arcs alone. A graph formed from the complete set of nodes but only a subset of the arcs A' is called a *partial graph* of (N, A). When the new graph is composed of a subset of the nodes N' and those arcs which have both nodes in N', it is called a *subgraph*. A *partial subgraph* is a combination of the two.

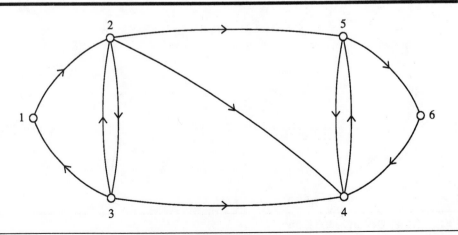

FIGURE 4-3   Chains, paths, cycles, and circuits.

Graphs may be connected or disconnected. A *connected* graph is one in which every pair of nodes is connected by a chain. A *disconnected* graph is one in which at least one pair of nodes exists that cannot be linked. A disconnected graph can be divided into *components* in which each component is a connected partial graph of the original graph. Figure 4-4 shows a disconnected graph with three components.

Connected and disconnected graphs are important to data communications. If a network is disconnected, there are nodes that will never receive information. For the simple examples shown here, ensuring that all nodes are connected is not difficult. As the number of nodes and arcs increases, however, ensuring connectivity can be more difficult.

A *tree* is a connected graph that contains no cycles. A *forest* is a graph with no cycles. Therefore, a forest is made up of trees. The concept of a tree is used often in determining the optimum way to connect a group of nodes. A *spanning tree* is a tree that connects all nodes in a network or graph.

Graphs and networks can be represented as matrices. These representations simplify some of the numerical operations when analyzing large networks. The two most common matrices are the *adjacency matrix* and the *incidence matrix.*

The adjacency matrix is a square matrix with one row and one column for each node. The values of the matrix are either 0 or 1. A value of 1 for row i, column j implies that arc (i, j) exists. A value of 0 implies there is no arc.

The incidence matrix, or node-arc matrix, consists of a row for every node and a column for every arc. The values of the matrix are -1, 0, or 1. If the kth arc is (i, j), the kth column has a value of 1 in the ith row, -1 in the jth row, and 0 elsewhere.

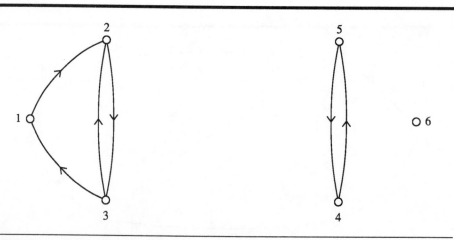

FIGURE 4-4   Disconnected graph.

Consider the graph shown in Figure 4-5. It consists of five nodes, $\{1, 2, 3, 4, 5\}$, and ten arcs, $\{(1, 2), (1, 3), (2, 1), (2, 3), (2, 5), (3, 1), (3, 4), (4, 1), (4, 5), (5, 3)\}$. The adjacency matrix and incidence matrix are:

$$\text{Adjacency Matrix} = \begin{bmatrix} 0 & 1 & 1 & 0 & 0 \\ 1 & 0 & 1 & 0 & 1 \\ 1 & 0 & 0 & 1 & 0 \\ 1 & 0 & 0 & 0 & 1 \\ 0 & 0 & 1 & 0 & 0 \end{bmatrix}$$

$$\text{Incidence Matrix} = \begin{bmatrix} 1 & 1 & -1 & 0 & 0 & -1 & 0 & -1 & 0 & 0 \\ -1 & 0 & 1 & 1 & 1 & 0 & 0 & 0 & 0 & 0 \\ 0 & -1 & 0 & -1 & 0 & 1 & 1 & 0 & 0 & -1 \\ 0 & 0 & 0 & 0 & 0 & 0 & -1 & 1 & 1 & 0 \\ 0 & 0 & 0 & 0 & -1 & 0 & 0 & 0 & -1 & 1 \end{bmatrix}$$

The properties of a graph or network are often listed in a similar matrix, with the value corresponding to the property. For example, the distance matrix corresponds to the distance of each arc. The distance matrix is the same as the adjacency matrix except that the zero values are now infinity (∞) and the non-zero values correspond to the length of the arc. An example distance matrix is

$$\text{Distance Matrix} = \begin{bmatrix} 0 & 2 & 3 & \infty & \infty \\ 2 & 0 & 1 & \infty & 5 \\ 3 & 0 & \infty & 1 & \infty \\ 1 & \infty & \infty & 0 & 2 \\ \infty & \infty & 3 & \infty & 0 \end{bmatrix}$$

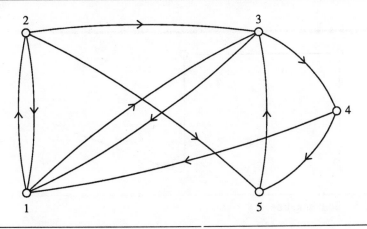

FIGURE 4-5 5-node, 10-arc graph.

Matrix representation presents a clear, but not necessarily concise, picture of a network. It is a useful means for storing a network configuration in a computer. But it is apparent that many of the values in the matrix convey little additional information. This is particularly true of the incidence matrix, in which all but two values in each column are 0. As the number of nodes and arcs increases, the memory requirements for a matrix representation gets very large. This is especially true when there is a property associated with each arc. For this reason, large networks are often stored as a list of nodes and a set of ordered pairs representing each arc. If there is a property associated with the arc, the ordered pair can become an ordered triple.

TREES

As stated above, trees are partial subgraphs that contain no cycles. A spanning tree contains every node in the graph. The spanning tree is "minimal" in the sense that every arc is necessary. If you add an arc to a spanning tree, it becomes cyclic and is no longer a tree. If you remove an arc, you still have a tree, but it no longer spans the graphs. At least one node is no longer connected. Figures 4-6, 4-7, and 4-8 demonstrate this process, using the graph from Figure 4-5.

If you associate a property with each arc, the graph (N, A) becomes the network (N, A, P). In trees, the properties of interest are ones that are additive. This means that if arc (i, j) has a property value of a and arc (j, k) has a property value of b, the value of the tree that connects the three nodes $i, j,$ and k is $a + b$.

The most common property is length. In data communications, however, the properties of cost or propagation time are more important. The tree of interest is

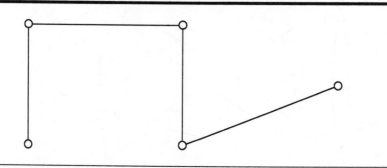

FIGURE 4-6   Spanning tree.

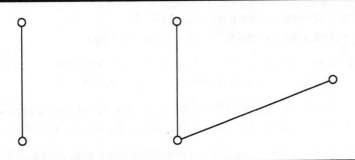

FIGURE 4-7   Non-spanning tree (arc deleted).

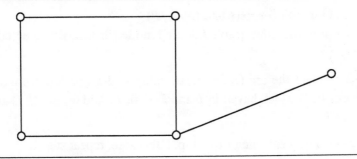

FIGURE 4-8   Non-tree (arcs added).

the one that minimizes the cost or length or propagation time of the network while connecting all the nodes. This tree is called the *minimal spanning tree.*

Construction of a minimal spanning tree is straightforward. It is obvious that the arcs in the tree must be the shortest arcs in the network with the smallest property values. By using an iterative procedure, you can start with the arc with the lowest value and then expand the tree using the available arcs with lowest values while ensuring that no cycles are formed.

The two primary ways of achieving this iteration were developed by J. B. Kruskal and R. C. Prim. Kruskal's method ranks all the arcs by value. The arcs are added in order of the value, smallest to largest. This method often results in many subtrees being grown simultaneously and then joined together. Prim's method, sometimes called the "greedy algorithm," starts at an arbitrarily selected node. At each stage of the algorithm, the arc that is the shortest arc remaining and has one vertex in tree is added. The formal algorithms for the two methods are as follows:

Kruskal's algorithm for network (N, A, P)

Step 1—Initialize the graph T with n nodes and no arcs.

Step 2—Create a list L of arcs from N in ascending order of their property value. Arcs with the same value are ranked arbitrarily.

Step 3—Select the arc (i, j) from the head of L. If it forms a circuit in T, delete it from L and repeat step 2. Otherwise transfer the arc from L to T.

Step 4—If T is a spanning tree, stop. Otherwise, repeat step 2.

Prim's algorithm for network (N, A, P)

Step 1—Initialize the graph T with 1 node (arbitrarily selected) and no arcs.

Step 2—Select the arc (i, j) whose value is the smallest from among those arcs (i, l) which have i in T and l not in T. Add the arc (i, j) and the node j to T.

Step 3—If T is a spanning tree, stop. Otherwise, repeat step 1.

To demonstrate the algorithms, consider a small computer network that consists of five nodes. You want to connect the five nodes at a minimal cost. You have cost estimates for each link.

At the outset of this problem, any link is possible, so a graph representing the network consists of five nodes with links between all the nodes. The adjacency matrix for such a graph is

$$
\text{Adjacency Matrix} =
\begin{bmatrix}
0 & 1 & 1 & 1 & 1 \\
1 & 0 & 1 & 1 & 1 \\
1 & 1 & 0 & 1 & 1 \\
1 & 1 & 1 & 0 & 1 \\
1 & 1 & 1 & 1 & 0
\end{bmatrix}
$$

The cost matrix assigns a cost of installation to each link. The values shown below are arbitrary. Also, the cost of installing a link over arc (i, j) is not necessarily equal to the cost of link over arc (j, i). The cost matrix is

$$\text{Cost Matrix} = \begin{bmatrix} \infty & 2 & 3 & 4 & 5 \\ 2 & \infty & 1 & 8 & 6 \\ 3 & 1 & \infty & 4 & 3 \\ 4 & 8 & 4 & \infty & 2 \\ 5 & 6 & 3 & 2 & \infty \end{bmatrix}$$

To implement the Kruskal algorithm, first initialize the graph T as ({1, 2, 3, 4, 5}, $\emptyset$). Then arrange the arcs in order of their distance value to form L = {(2, 3), (1, 2), (4, 5), (1, 3), (3, 5), (1, 4), (3, 4), (1, 5), (2, 5), (2, 4)}. Now iterate, adding the shortest arc that does not make a circuit.

After three steps, T is ({1, 2, 3, 4, 5}, {(2, 3), (1, 2), (4, 5)}) and L is {(1, 3), (3, 5), (1, 4), (3, 4), (1, 5), (2, 5), (2, 4)}. If (1, 3) is added to T, a circuit would be formed. The fourth step, therefore, drops (1, 3) from L without adding it to T. The next step adds (3, 5) to T, forming the minimal spanning tree, T = ({1, 2, 3, 4, 5}, {(2, 3), (1, 2), (4, 5), (3, 5)}). The value of T is 1 + 2 + 2 + 3 = 8.

The Prim algorithm starts with the selection of an arbitrary node. For this example, assume that 5 is the initial node. Then T is ({5}, $\emptyset$). The smallest arc connected to node 5 is (4, 5) so T becomes ({4, 5}, {(4, 5)}). The smallest arc connected to nodes 4 or 5 is (3, 5). T becomes ({3, 4, 5}, {(3, 5), (4, 5)}). The next two steps add first arc (2, 3) and then arc (1, 2). Finally, T = ({1, 2, 3, 4, 5}, {(1, 2), (2, 3), (3, 5), (4, 5)}).

Figure 4-9 on the following page shows the construction of the minimal spanning tree step by step. In this particular case, the two minimal trees are identical. The two algorithms do not necessarily provide a unique tree, simply the minimal spanning tree. As the number of nodes and links increase, it is very probable that multiple minimal spanning trees will exist.

Both the Kruskal and Prim algorithms can be used to find the *maximal spanning tree*. This is the spanning tree with the maximal value. The only difference is that the arc with the maximal value is chosen each time. For the previous example, the maximal spanning tree is T = ({1, 2, 3, 4, 5}, {(1, 5), (2, 5), (2, 4), (3, 4)}). The maximal value is 23.

As stated above, the property value associated with the minimal or maximal spanning tree can be any real number that is additive as arcs are joined. A measure of network reliability can be obtained by letting the property value represent the log of the probability that the link will transmit the message successfully. Assuming that the probability for each arc is independent of every other arc, the maximal spanning tree represents the chain with the highest probability of success. The probability of success is antilog ("length" of the minimal tree).

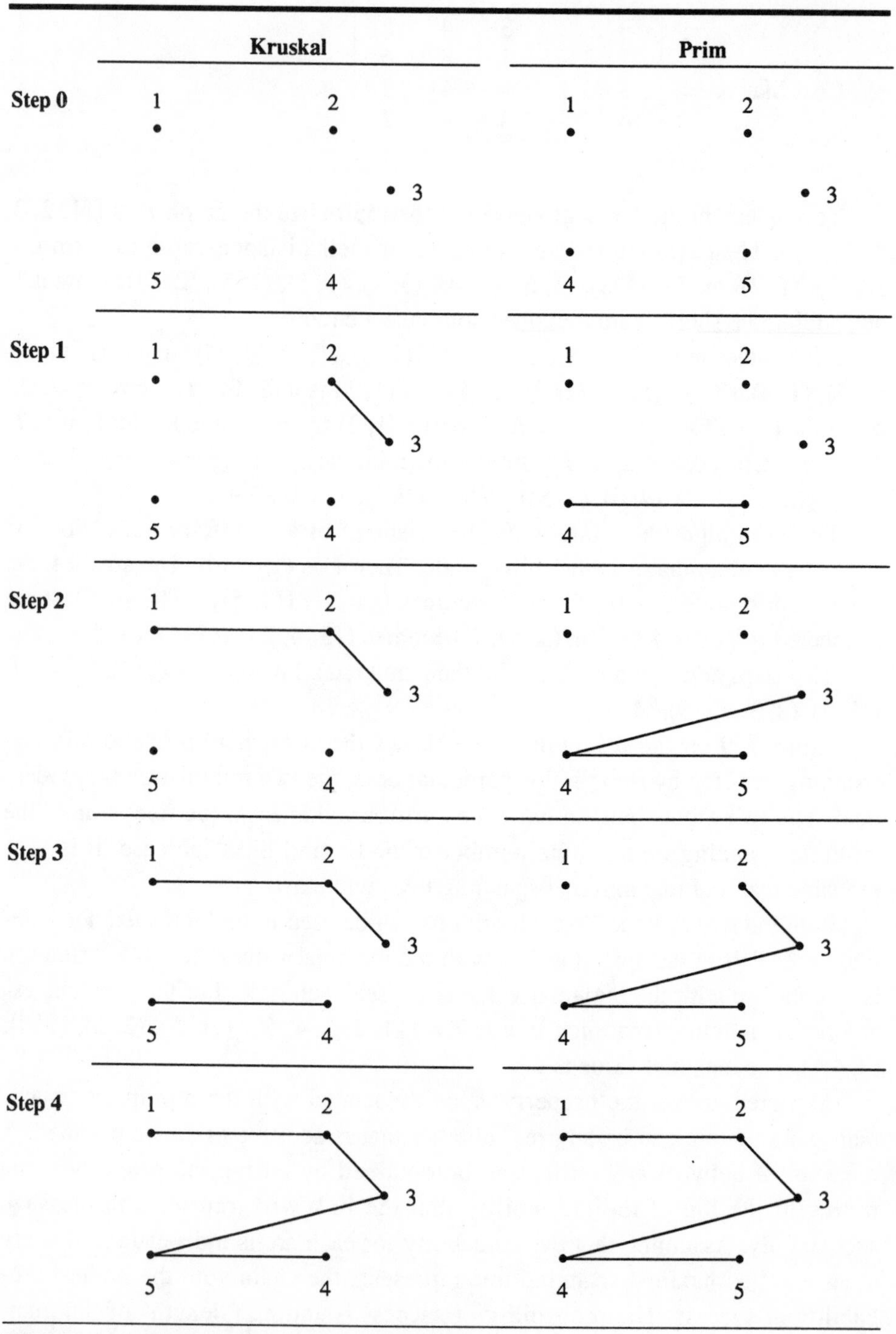

FIGURE 4-9   Minimal spanning tree construction.

CONNECTEDNESS

The idea of connectedness is very easy to determine from a diagram. An unconnected node stands out very clearly. But when the number of nodes and arcs is very large and the representation is via a large adjacency matrix or a long series of ordered pairs, it is not as clear. The simplest algorithm for determining whether a graph is connected uses the adjacency matrix.

As noted earlier, the adjacency matrix is an n by n matrix where n is the number of nodes. If you square the adjacency matrix, its entries correspond to the number of different paths between two nodes that use two arcs. Cubing the matrix yields the number of 3-arc paths between node i and j in the (i, j) position. If a graph is connected, it is possible to find a path between every pair of nodes that uses at most $n - 1$ arcs.

To test for connectedness, determine the sum $Y = X + X^2 + \cdots + X^{n-1}$. The matrix Y will have zero entries for any nodes that are not connected. If no zeros exist in Y, the graph is connected. The sum matrix Y also has the property of indicating the components of an unconnected graph, similar to reduction of Markov chains to closed sets discussed in Chapter 2.

The obvious problem with this algorithm is that as n increases, the computational burden of taking the n by n matrix to the $n - 1$ power becomes burdensome. An alternate algorithm is based on creating a "connectedness matrix" by addition of rows and columns of the adjacency matrix.

The connectedness matrix is similar to the adjacency matrix in that its entries are 0 or 1. The ith row contains an entry of 1 for each node, which i is connected to, regardless of how many arcs are involved in getting there. The matrix is built up from the adjacency matrix using the principle that if i is connected to j and j is connected to k, then i is connected to k.

This can be expressed in terms of logical addition of the jth row to the ith row and the jth column to the ith column, followed by the deletion of the jth row and column. In logical addition, $0 + 0 = 0$ and $0 + 1 = 1 + 0 = 1 + 1 = 1$. To test for connectedness, the rules are applied to node 1 until either all the other rows and columns have been deleted or no other ones can be deleted. If all other rows and columns are deleted, the graph is connected. The formal steps for this algorithm are as follows.

Connectedness Algorithm
Step 1—Initialize X as the adjacency matrix. Set $i = 1$ and $c = 0$.

Step 2—Find $X_{ij} \neq 0$ ($j > i$). Logically add row j to row i, column j to column i. Delete row j and column j from X. If no j exists, go to step 3. Otherwise repeat Step 1.

Step 3—Set $c = c + 1$. Find $k > i$ such that row k has not been deleted. If no such k exists, then stop. The graph has c components. Otherwise, set $i = k$ and go to step 2.

To demonstrate a possible use of the connectedness algorithms consider a telephone network where, by initial design, two-way links exist between all pairs of nodes. This network has the same adjacency matrix as the previous example,

$$X = \begin{bmatrix} 0 & 1 & 1 & 1 & 1 \\ 1 & 0 & 1 & 1 & 1 \\ 1 & 1 & 0 & 1 & 1 \\ 1 & 1 & 1 & 0 & 1 \\ 1 & 1 & 1 & 1 & 0 \end{bmatrix}$$

Although this network is obviously connected, it is instructional to work through the algorithm. Following the steps, set $i = 1$ and $c = 0$. Then note that $X_{12} = 1 \neq 0$. Logically adding the first and second rows and columns yields

$$X = \begin{bmatrix} 1 & 1 & 1 & 1 & 1 \\ 1 & 0 & 1 & 1 & 1 \\ 1 & 1 & 0 & 1 & 1 \\ 1 & 1 & 1 & 0 & 1 \\ 1 & 1 & 1 & 1 & 0 \end{bmatrix}$$

Then deleting the second row and column produces

$$X = \begin{bmatrix} 1 & - & 1 & 1 & 1 \\ - & - & - & - & - \\ 1 & - & 0 & 1 & 1 \\ 1 & - & 1 & 0 & 1 \\ 1 & - & 1 & 1 & 0 \end{bmatrix}$$

Repeating Step 2, note that again $X_{13} = 1 \neq 0$. Logically adding the first and third rows and columns yields

$$X = \begin{bmatrix} 1 & - & 1 & 1 & 1 \\ - & - & - & - & - \\ 1 & - & 0 & 1 & 1 \\ 1 & - & 1 & 0 & 1 \\ 1 & - & 1 & 1 & 0 \end{bmatrix}$$

Deleting the third column and row produces

$$X = \begin{bmatrix} 1 & - & - & 1 & 1 \\ - & - & - & - & - \\ - & - & - & - & - \\ 1 & - & - & 0 & 1 \\ 1 & - & - & 1 & 0 \end{bmatrix}$$

Repeating the process two more times yields

$$X = \begin{bmatrix} 1 & - & - & - & - \\ - & - & - & - & - \\ - & - & - & - & - \\ - & - & - & - & - \\ - & - & - & - & - \end{bmatrix}$$

Now, after a severe storm in the area, a number of the links have been knocked out. You need to determine if all nodes are still connected. The arcs that were eliminated are now zeros in the adjacency matrix. The new adjacency matrix is

$$X = \begin{bmatrix} 0 & 1 & 0 & 0 & 0 \\ 1 & 0 & 0 & 0 & 1 \\ 0 & 0 & 0 & 1 & 0 \\ 0 & 0 & 1 & 0 & 0 \\ 0 & 1 & 0 & 0 & 0 \end{bmatrix}$$

After the first two steps, the matrix becomes

$$X = \begin{bmatrix} 1 & - & 0 & 0 & - \\ 0 & - & 0 & 1 & - \\ 0 & - & 1 & 0 & - \\ - & - & - & - & - \end{bmatrix}$$

At this point, there is no $X_{1j} \neq 0$. Therefore, increment c by 1 and set $k = i = 3$. Then $X_{34} = 1 \neq 0$. Updating the matrix produces

$$X = \begin{bmatrix} 1 & - & 0 & - & - \\ 0 & - & 1 & - & - \\ 0 & - & - & - & - \\ - & - & - & - & - \end{bmatrix}$$

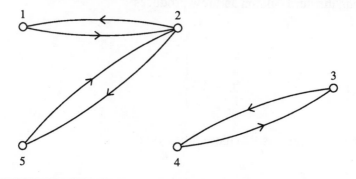

FIGURE 4-10   Non-connected graph with two components.

There are no further $X_{3j} \neq 0$, so c is incremented to 2. Because no further k exists, the process stops. The network now has two disconnected components, as demonstrated in Figure 4-10.

OPTIMAL PATHS

Mathematics is always concerned with finding the best way to do something. Routing messages through a complex network is no exception. A considerable amount of network theory is devoted to determining the *optimal path* through the network. As in the case of the tree, optimal can be used in a variety of ways. Typical values that are optimized are length of the path, the propagation time of the path, and the cost of the path.

Note that in this discussion it is a path that is optimized. The previous discussion concerned a tree. The fact that a tree connects a group of nodes does not mean that a path exists between the nodes. Remember that a path is a tree with no reverse arcs. If a tree contains a reverse arc, it is not a path.

For purposes of discussion, the optimal path is assumed to represent length. The approach is to introduce three algorithms in three increasing levels of complexity. The simplest algorithm is *Dijkstra's algorithm*. It is used to determine the shortest path between two arbitrary nodes on a network. *Ford's algorithm* determines the shortest path between a single node and all other nodes in the network. *Floyd's algorithm* finds the shortest paths between all pairs of nodes.

Dijkstra's Algorithm

Assume that there is a distance $d(i, j)$ associated with every arc (i, j) in a given network. Furthermore, the distances are such that the distance from node i to node k via node j is $d(i, j) + d(j, k)$. Using this technique, the distance from a node s (the start of the path) to node t (the end of the path or terminus) in the network N, given a path $(s, i_1), (i_1, i_2), (i_2, i_3), \ldots, (i_p, t)$ is given by $d(s, i_1) + d(i_1, i_2) + d(i_2, i_3) + \cdots + d(i_p, t)$. In a complex network, there are many possible paths between s and t. Although many methods exist for finding the shortest path, the Dijkstra method is the mostly widely used and one of the more efficient algorithms.

The first step is to ensure that there is a distance associated with every pair of nodes in the network. If there is indeed an arc between two nodes, the distance is the arc length. If several arcs exist, use the one with shortest length. If no arc actually exists, set the length to infinity. Arc (i, j) does not necessarily have to have the same length as arc (j, i). This allows for different routes between two arcs that take different paths depending on the direction of travel. This is analogous to a series of one-way streets in a city.

Dijkstra's method is based on assigning labels to each node. The label is equal to the distance from the start node to that node. Obviously, the start node, s, has a label of 0. In addition to its value, a label can be in one of two states, temporary or permanent. A permanent label is one that lies along the shortest path. A temporary label is one that has some uncertainty as to whether the label is along the shortest path. (Different texts refer to permanent and temporary labels as colored and uncolored labels or permanent and tentative labels.)

The algorithm gradually changes the temporary labels to permanent labels until the end node t has a permanent label. At each step, the aim is to make the temporary labels shorter by finding paths to the associated nodes using the shortest paths to the permanently labeled nodes. After this is done, the temporary label with the smallest value is made permanent. This process eliminates one temporary node at each step, ensuring that the shortest path from s to t will eventually be found. Notice that if no path exists from s to t, the shortest path will be infinity. Formally stated, Dijkstra's algorithm is as follows:

Dijkstra's Algorithm for Shortest Path

Step 1—Assign a temporary label $l(i) = \infty$ to all nodes except s. Set $l(s) = 0$. Denote $l(s)$ as a permanent label. Set $r = s$ (r is the last node to be made permanent).

Step 2—For each node i with a temporary label, redefine $l(i)$ to be the smaller of $l(i)$ and $l(p) + d(p, i)$. Then find the node i with the smallest temporary label, make the label permanent, and set $r = i$.

Step 3—If node t has a temporary label, repeat step 2. Otherwise the value of t's permanent label is equal to the shortest path from s to t.

To demonstrate the algorithm in use, consider a telecommunications network that can be described by the graph in Figure 4-5. The network consists of 5 nodes and 10 arcs. You want to send a message from node 1 to node 5 over the shortest possible route. The distance matrix associated with this network is

$$
\text{Distance Matrix} =
\begin{bmatrix}
0 & 2 & 3 & \infty & \infty \\
2 & 0 & 1 & \infty & 5 \\
3 & 0 & \infty & 1 & \infty \\
1 & \infty & \infty & 0 & 2 \\
\infty & \infty & 3 & \infty & 0
\end{bmatrix}
$$

Let node 1 be s and node 5 be t. A cursory visual examination of this simple example indicates that there are two possible paths, node 1 to 2 to 5 and node 1 to 2 to 3 to 4 to 5. The distance in the first path is 7, the distance in the latter path is 6. But now use Dijkstra's algorithm to determine the same result.

• **Step 1**—Assign labels as in the table below. Set $r = s = 1$ and make $l(s)$ permanent.

	s	2	3	4	t
$l(\ )$	0	∞	∞	∞	∞
permanent?	yes	no	no	no	no

• **Step 2**—Redefine the temporary labels as follows:

$l(2) = \min(\infty, 0 + 2) = 2$
$l(3) = \min(\infty, 0 + 3) = 3$
$l(4) = \min(\infty, 0 + \infty) = \infty$
$l(t) = \min(\infty, 0 + \infty) = \infty$

Make $l(2)$ permanent. Set $r = 2$.

	s	2	3	4	t
$l(\ )$	0	2	∞	∞	∞
permanent?	yes	yes	no	no	no

• **Step 3**—Repeat Step 2.
• **Step 2**—Redefine the temporary labels as follows:

$l(3) = \min(3, 2 + 1) = 3$
$l(4) = \min(\infty, 2 + \infty) = \infty$
$l(t) = \min(\infty, 2 + 5) = 7$

Make $l(3)$ permanent. Set $r = 3$.

	s	2	3	4	t
$l(\ )$	0	2	3	∞	∞
permanent?	yes	yes	yes	no	no

- **Step 3**—Repeat Step 2.
- **Step 2**—Redefine the temporary labels as follows:

$l(4) = \min(\infty, 3 + 1) = 4$
$l(t) = \min(7, 3 + \infty) = 7$

Make $l(4)$ permanent. Set $r = 4$.

	s	2	3	4	t
$l(\ )$	0	2	3	4	∞
permanent?	yes	yes	yes	yes	no

- **Step 3**—Repeat Step 2.
- **Step 2**—Redefine the temporary labels as follows:

$l(t) = \min(7, 4 + 2) = 6$

Make $l(t)$ permanent. Set $r = t$.

	s	2	3	4	t
$l(\ )$	0	2	3	4	6
permanent?	yes	yes	yes	yes	yes

- **Step 3**—$l(t)$ is permanent. The shortest path length is 6.

Notice that in this example all nodes now have permanent labels. When this occurs, the value of each label represents the shortest distance from s to the designated node. In general, Dijkstra's algorithm does not always assign a permanent label to all nodes before determining the shortest path to node t. For example, if node 3 is selected as t, the final labels are

	s	2	t	4	5
$l(\ )$	0	2	3	∞	∞
permanent?	yes	yes	yes	no	no

The original algorithm can be altered easily so that all the shortest distances to all nodes are determined by altering the stop condition in step 3. The new step 3 becomes:

Step 3—If *any* node has a temporary label, repeat step 2. Otherwise, all nodes have permanent labels, and the value of the permanent label is equal to the shortest path from *s* to the node.

To demonstrate the modified algorithm, find the shortest distance from node 3 to all other nodes. For simplicity, rearrange the order of the nodes.

- **Step 1**—Assign labels as in the table below. For simplicity, rearrange the order of the nodes. Set $r = s = 3$ and make $l(s)$ permanent.

	s	1	2	4	5
$l(\ )$	0	∞	∞	∞	∞
permanent?	yes	no	no	no	no

- **Step 2**—Redefine the temporary labels as follows:

$l(1) = \min(\infty, 0 + 3) = 3$
$l(2) = \min(\infty, 0 + \infty) = \infty$
$l(4) = \min(\infty, 0 + 1) = 1$
$l(5) = \min(\infty, 0 + \infty) = \infty$

Make $l(4)$ permanent. Set $r = 4$.

	s	1	2	4	5
$l(\ )$	0	3	∞	1	∞
permanent?	yes	no	no	yes	no

- **Step 3**—Repeat Step 2.
- **Step 2**—Redefine the temporary labels as follows:

$l(1) = \min(3, 1 + 1) = 2$
$l(2) = \min(\infty, 1 + \infty) = \infty$
$l(5) = \min(\infty, 1 + 2) = 3$

Make $l(1)$ permanent. Set $r = 1$.

	s	1	2	4	5
$l(\ )$	0	2	∞	1	3
permanent?	yes	yes	no	yes	no

• **Step 3**—Repeat Step 2.
• **Step 2**—Redefine the temporary labels as follows:

$l(2) = \min(\infty, 2 + 2) = 4$
$l(5) = \min(3, 3 + \infty) = 3$

Make $l(5)$ permanent. Set $r = 5$.

	s	1	2	4	5
$l(\ )$	0	2	4	1	3
permanent?	yes	yes	no	yes	yes

• **Step 3**—Repeat Step 2.
• **Step 2**—Redefine the temporary labels as follows:

$l(2) = \min(4, 4 + \infty) = 4$

Make $l(2)$ permanent. Set $r = 2$.

	s	1	2	4	5
$l(\ )$	0	2	4	1	3
permanent?	yes	yes	yes	yes	yes

• **Step 3**—All labels are permanent. The shortest paths are shown.

This example demonstrates a potential weakness in the algorithm. Although you know the shortest distance from a designated node for every other node, you do not necessarily know what path was taken. The algorithm as currently constructed provides no indication of the composition of the optimal path.

One method for determining the composition of the shortest path is to assign a second label to each node, denoted as $p(i)$. $p(i)$ contains the predecessor node in the path whose length is $l(i)$. Whenever $l(i)$ assumes a smaller value, the predecessor node is changed. Implementing this change requires a modification of step 2.

Step 2—For each node i with a temporary label, redefine $l(i)$ to be the smaller of $l(i)$ and $l(r) + d(r, i)$. If $l(i) > l(r) + d(r, i)$, set $p(i) = r$. Then find the node i with the smallest temporary label, make the label permanent, and set $r = i$.

The previous example is repeated below, this time determining the composition of the shortest path.

• **Step 1**—Assign labels as in the table below. Set $r = s = 3$ and make $l(s)$ permanent. At this point, no nodes have predecessors so all the $p(i)$ are undefined.

	s	1	2	4	5
$l(\ )$	0	∞	∞	∞	∞
$p(\ )$	–	–	–	–	–
permanent?	yes	no	no	no	no

• **Step 2**—Redefine the temporary labels as follows:

$l(1) = \min(\infty, 0 + 3) = 3$
$l(2) = \min(\infty, 0 + \infty) = \infty$
$l(4) = \min(\infty, 0 + 1) = 1$
$l(5) = \min(\infty, 0 + \infty) = \infty$

Make $l(4)$ permanent. Set $p(1) = p(4) = r = 3$ because $l(1)$ and $l(4)$ assumed smaller values in this step. Set $r = 4$.

	s	1	2	4	5
$l(\ )$	0	3	∞	1	∞
$p(\ )$	–	3	–	3	–
permanent?	yes	no	no	yes	no

• **Step 3**—Repeat Step 2.
• **Step 2**—Redefine the temporary labels as follows:

$l(1) = \min(3, 1 + 1) = 2$
$l(2) = \min(\infty, 1 + \infty) = \infty$
$l(5) = \min(\infty, 1 + 2) = 3$

Make $l(1)$ permanent. Set $p(1) = p(5) = r = 4$. Again, these values of $n(\ )$ are changed because the corresponding value of $l(\ )$ is lowered in this step. Set $r = 1$.

	s	1	2	4	5
$l(\ )$	0	2	–	1	3
$p(\ )$	–	4	3	3	4
permanent?	yes	yes	no	yes	no

- **Step 3**—Repeat Step 2.
- **Step 2**—Redefine the temporary labels as follows:

$l(2) = \min(\infty, 2 + 2) = 4$
$l(5) = \min(3, 3 + \infty) = 3$

Make $l(5)$ permanent. Set $p(2) = r = 1$. Set $r = 5$.

	s	1	2	4	5
$l(\ )$	0	2	4	1	3
$p(\ )$	–	4	1	3	4
permanent?	yes	yes	no	yes	yes

- **Step 3**—Repeat Step 2.
- **Step 2**—Redefine the temporary labels as follows:

$l(2) = \min(4, 4 + \infty) = 4$

Make $l(2)$ permanent. Set $r = 2$

	s	1	2	4	5
$l(\ )$	0	2	4	1	3
$p(\ )$	–	4	1	3	4
permanent?	yes	yes	yes	yes	yes

- **Step 3**—All labels are permanent. The shortest path lengths are shown.

The shortest paths are determined by following the connections. The only node whose shortest path is a direct connection to node 3 is node 4. The shortest path to nodes 1 and 5 goes from node 3 to node 4 and then to node 1 or 5. The shortest path to node 2 goes from node 3 to node 4 to node 1 to node 2.

Ford's Algorithm

Dijkstra's algorithm is very well suited to cases in which the quantity that is to be optimized is always a positive value. If the cost of each arc in the network is positive, the algorithm will find the minimal cost path. There are cases, however, in which the cost of one or more arcs may be negative. In this case, using the negative cost arcs shows a profit. Ford developed an algorithm very similar to Dijkstra's that allows negative cost arcs.

Ford's algorithm finds the lowest cost path over a network that includes negative cost arcs, provided that no circuits exist around which there is a negative cost. If such a circuit did exist, it could be looped around indefinitely to produce an arbitrarily low cost. Ford's algorithm has the additional advantage that the permanent/temporary state of the labels no longer needs to be monitored.

The algorithm assigns labels to each node, which represent the shortest path found to the node thus far. On each iteration, a search is made for a label that can be reduced, using the same approach as in Dijkstra's method. The algorithm ends when no labels can be reduced. Formally, the algorithm is as follows:

Ford's Algorithm For Shortest Path with Negative Costs

Step 1—Assign a label $l(i) = \infty$ to each node in the network. Set $l(s) = 0$.

Step 2—For each node j, test to see if there is an arc (i, j) such that $l(i) + d(i, j) < l(j)$. If such an arc exists, go to step 3. If no arc exists, stop.

Step 3—Change $l(j)$ to $l(i) + d(i, j)$. Repeat Step 2.

On termination, the $l(t)$ is the shortest path from s to t. The actual path from s to t can be determined using the same method used in Dijkstra's algorithm.

As noted above, the algorithm fails if the network includes a negative cost circuit. The first step to preventing this is to exclude any two-way arcs that have a negative cost. Larger circuits can be harder to find, especially in a complex network. Fortunately, it is easy to determine if a negative cost circuit exists. Once its existence is known, the algorithm can be stopped.

The existence of a negative cost circuit is determined when a node's label continues to change indefinitely. If the number of changes reaches n, the number of nodes in the network, then a negative cost circuit exists. This check is implemented in the algorithm by limiting the times step 2 is repeated for a single node j to $n - 1$.

To demonstrate the algorithm, once again consider the network shown in Figure 4-5. But rather than a distance matrix, consider a cost matrix that includes some negative costs:

$$
\text{Cost Matrix} = \begin{bmatrix}
0 & 7 & 8 & \infty & \infty \\
-3 & 0 & 5 & \infty & 6 \\
4 & 0 & \infty & -2 & \infty \\
4 & \infty & \infty & 0 & -2 \\
\infty & \infty & 7 & \infty & 0
\end{bmatrix}
$$

Ford's algorithm is implemented in the following steps. The process of determining the composition of the lowest cost path is omitted.

- **Step 1**—Assign labels as in the table below. Set $p = s = 1$ and $l(s) = 0$.

	s	2	3	4	t
$l(\,)$	0	∞	∞	∞	∞

- **Step 2**—Test node s: $l(i) + d(i, s) \geq \neq l(s)$ for all i.
  —Test node 2: $l(s) + d(s, 2) < l(2)$. Do step 3.
- **Step 3**—Change label on node 2.

	s	2	3	4	t
$l(\,)$	0	7	∞	∞	∞

- **Step 2**—Test node s: $l(i) + d(i, s) \geq \neq l(s)$ for all i.
  —Test node 2: $l(i) + d(i, 2) \geq \neq l(2)$ for all i.
  —Test node 3: $l(s) + d(s, 3) < l(3)$.
- **Step 3**—Change label on node 3.

	s	2	3	4	5
$l(\,)$	0	7	8	∞	∞

- **Step 2**—Test node s: $l(i) + d(i, s) \geq \neq l(s)$ for all i.
  —Test node 2: $l(i) + d(i, 2) \geq \neq l(2)$ for all i.
  —Test node 3: $l(2) + d(2, 3) < l(3)$. Repeat step.

- **Step 2**—Test node s: $l(i) + d(i, s) \geq \neq l(s)$ for all i.
  —Test node 2: $l(i) + d(i, 2) \geq \neq l(2)$ for all i.
  —Test node 5: $l(5) + d(2, 5) < l(5)$. Repeat step.
- **Step 3**—Change label on node 5.

	s	2	3	4	5
$l(\,)$	0	7	8	∞	13

- **Step 2**—Test node s: $l(i) + d(i, s) \geq \neq l(s)$ for all i.
  —Test node 2: $l(i) + d(i, 2) \geq \neq l(2)$ for all i.
  —Test node 3: $l(i) + d(i, 3) \geq \neq l(3)$ for all i.
  —Test node 4: $l(s) + d(s, 4) < l(4)$. Repeat step.

- **Step 2**—Test node s: $l(i) + d(i, s) \geq \neq l(s)$ for all i.
  —Test node 2: $l(i) + d(i, 2) \geq \neq l(2)$ for all i.
  —Test node 3: $l(i) + d(i, 3) \geq \neq l(3)$ for all i.
  —Test node 4: $l(2) + d(2, 4) < l(4)$. Repeat step.

- **Step 2**—Test node s: $l(i) + d(i, s) \geq \neq l(s)$ for all i.
  —Test node 2: $l(i) + d(i, 2) \geq \neq l(2)$ for all i.
  —Test node 3: $l(i) + d(i, 3) \geq \neq l(3)$ for all i.
  —Test node 4: $l(3) + d(3, 4) < l(4)$. Do step 3.
- **Step 3**—Change label on node 4.

$l(\ )$	s	2	3	4	5
	0	7	8	6	13

- **Step 2**—Test node s: $l(i) + d(i, s) \geq \neq l(s)$ for all i.
  —Test node 2: $l(i) + d(i, 2) \geq \neq l(2)$ for all i.
  —Test node 3: $l(i) + d(i, 3) \geq \neq l(3)$ for all i.
  —Test node 4: $l(i) + d(i, 4) \geq \neq l(4)$ for all i.
  —Test node 5: $l(s) + d(s, 5) < l(5)$. Repeat step.

- **Step 2**—Test node s: $l(i) + d(i, s) \geq \neq l(s)$ for all i.
  —Test node 2: $l(i) + d(i, 2) \geq \neq l(2)$ for all i.
  —Test node 3: $l(i) + d(i, 3) \geq \neq l(3)$ for all i.
  —Test node 4: $l(i) + d(i, 4) \geq \neq l(4)$ for all i.
  —Test node 5: $l(4) + d(4, 5) < l(5)$. Do step 3.
- **Step 3**—Change label on node 5.

$l(\ )$	s	2	3	4	t
	0	7	8	6	4

- **Step 2**—Test node s: $l(i) + d(i, s) \geq \neq l(s)$ for all i.
  —Test node 2: $l(i) + d(i, 2) \geq \neq l(2)$ for all i.
  —Test node 3: $l(i) + d(i, 3) \geq \neq l(3)$ for all i.
  —Test node 4: $l(i) + d(i, 4) \geq \neq l(4)$ for all i.
  —Test node 5: $l(i) + d(i, 5) \geq \neq l(5)$ for all i.
  —No change to any label. Stop.

From this, the lowest cost paths from node 1 to nodes 2, 3, 4, and 5 are 7, 8, 6, and 4 respectively.

Floyd's Algorithm

Both Dijkstra's and Ford's algorithms will find the shortest path between s and all the other nodes. If the algorithms are repeated n times, with a different s each time, shortest paths between every pair of nodes in the network can be determined. This process can be tedious. Floyd developed an algorithm that solves the problem of determining all shortest paths in a somewhat more succinct fashion.

Floyd's algorithm starts by numbering each node from 1 to n. The algorithm uses the distance matrix to first find the shortest paths that are either direct or use node 1 and an intermediate node. Then it finds the shortest paths that used node 1 and/or node 2 as intermediate nodes. The process continues until the shortest paths are found that either are direct or use some or all of the nodes 1 to n as intermediate nodes.

The distances found are the intermediate steps in the process and are stored in an n by n matrix D_k whose elements $d_k(i, j)$ represent the shortest distance between nodes i and j when nodes 1 through k are used as intermediate nodes. The elements $d_{k+1}(i, j)$ are either $d_k(i, j)$ (if there is no advantage to including node k in the path) or $d_k(i, k+1) + d_k(k+1, j)$ (if including node k shortens the path). The matrix D_n contains all the shortest paths. D_0 is the distance matrix.

As in the Dijkstra and Ford methods, it is useful to keep track of the composition of the shortest path. This is done by including an evaluation of the preceding node in the algorithm and maintaining an n by n matrix P. The predecessor of node t in the shortest path from s to t is the node k that satisfies $d_n(s, t) = d_n(s, k) + d(k, t)$. The formal algorithm is as follows:

Floyd's Algorithm for all Shortest Paths

Step 1—Create the n by n matrix D_0 as the distance matrix. Create the n by n matrix P with elements $p(i, j) = i$. Set $k = 0$.

Step 2—Create the n by n matrix D_{k+1} with elements $d_{k+1}(i, j) = \min \times \{d_k(i, j), d_k(i, k+1) + d_k(k+1, j)\}$. If $d_{k+1}(i, j) < d_k(i, j)$, set $p(i, j) = p(k+1, j)$.

Step 3—Set $k = k + 1$. If $k = n$, stop. Otherwise, repeat step 2.

To demonstrate this process, revisit the communication network described in Figure 4-5. For the network to operate effectively, each node needs to know the shortest path to use when routing messages through the network. Actually, the node does not need to know the complete route from itself to node j. It just needs to know what node k the message should be sent to next to continue on the shortest path from itself to node j. This information is contained in the P matrix as defined above. To start the process, D_0 and P are initialized as described above.

• **Step 1**

$$D_0 = \begin{bmatrix} 0 & 2 & 3 & \infty & \infty \\ 2 & 0 & 1 & \infty & 5 \\ 3 & \infty & 0 & 1 & \infty \\ 1 & \infty & \infty & 0 & 2 \\ \infty & \infty & 3 & \infty & 0 \end{bmatrix}$$

$$P = \begin{bmatrix} 1 & 1 & 1 & 1 & 1 \\ 2 & 2 & 2 & 2 & 2 \\ 3 & 3 & 3 & 3 & 3 \\ 4 & 4 & 4 & 4 & 4 \\ 5 & 5 & 5 & 5 & 5 \end{bmatrix}$$

$$k = 0$$

• **Step 2**

$d_1(1, 1) = \min(0, 0 + 0) = 0$ $p(1, 1) = 1$
$d_1(1, 2) = \min(2, 0 + 2) = 2$ $p(1, 2) = 1$
$d_1(1, 3) = \min(3, 0 + 3) = 3$ $p(1, 3) = 1$
$d_1(1, 4) = \min(\infty, 0 + \infty) = \infty$ $p(1, 4) = 1$
$d_1(1, 5) = \min(\infty, 0 + \infty) = \infty$ $p(1, 5) = 1$

$d_1(2, 1) = \min(2, 2 + 0) = 2$ $p(2, 1) = 2$
$d_1(2, 2) = \min(0, 2 + 2) = 0$ $p(2, 2) = 2$
$d_1(2, 3) = \min(1, 2 + 3) = 1$ $p(2, 3) = 2$
$d_1(2, 4) = \min(\infty, 2 + \infty) = \infty$ $p(2, 4) = 2$
$d_1(2, 5) = \min(5, 2 + \infty) = 5$ $p(2, 5) = 2$

$d_1(3, 1) = \min(3, 3 + 0) = 3$ $p(3, 1) = 3$
$d_1(3, 2) = \min(\infty, 3 + 2) = 5$ $p(3, 2) = 1$
$d_1(3, 3) = \min(0, 3 + 3) = 0$ $p(3, 3) = 3$
$d_1(3, 4) = \min(1, 3 + \infty) = 1$ $p(3, 4) = 3$
$d_1(3, 5) = \min(\infty, 3 + \infty) = \infty$ $p(3, 5) = 3$

$d_1(4, 1) = \min(1, \infty + 0) = 1$ $p(4, 1) = 4$
$d_1(4, 2) = \min(\infty, \infty + 2) = \infty$ $p(4, 2) = 4$
$d_1(4, 3) = \min(\infty, \infty + 3) = \infty$ $p(4, 3) = 4$
$d_1(4, 4) = \min(0, \infty + \infty) = 0$ $p(4, 4) = 4$
$d_1(4, 5) = \min(2, \infty + \infty) = 2$ $p(4, 5) = 4$

$$d_1(5, 1) = \min(\infty, \infty + 0) = \infty \qquad p(5, 1) = 5$$
$$d_1(5, 2) = \min(\infty, \infty + 2) = \infty \qquad p(5, 2) = 5$$
$$d_1(5, 3) = \min(3, \infty + 3) = 3 \qquad p(5, 3) = 5$$
$$d_1(5, 4) = \min(\infty, \infty + \infty) = \infty \qquad p(5, 4) = 5$$
$$d_1(5, 5) = \min(0, \infty + \infty) = 0 \qquad p(5, 5) = 5$$

So now

$$D_1 = \begin{bmatrix} 0 & 2 & 3 & \infty & \infty \\ 2 & 0 & 1 & \infty & 5 \\ 3 & 5 & 0 & 1 & \infty \\ 1 & \infty & \infty & 0 & 2 \\ \infty & \infty & 3 & \infty & 0 \end{bmatrix}$$

$$P = \begin{bmatrix} 1 & 1 & 1 & 1 & 1 \\ 2 & 2 & 2 & 2 & 2 \\ 3 & 1 & 3 & 3 & 3 \\ 4 & 4 & 4 & 4 & 4 \\ 5 & 5 & 5 & 5 & 5 \end{bmatrix}$$

• **Step 3**—$k = 1$ (not equal to 5). Do Step 2.
• **Step 2**—Using the same method, calculate D_2 and P:

$$D_2 = \begin{bmatrix} 0 & 2 & 3 & \infty & 7 \\ 2 & 0 & 1 & \infty & 5 \\ 3 & 5 & 0 & 1 & 10 \\ 1 & \infty & \infty & 0 & 2 \\ \infty & \infty & 3 & \infty & 0 \end{bmatrix}$$

$$P = \begin{bmatrix} 1 & 1 & 1 & 1 & 2 \\ 2 & 2 & 2 & 2 & 2 \\ 3 & 1 & 3 & 3 & 2 \\ 4 & 4 & 4 & 4 & 4 \\ 5 & 5 & 5 & 5 & 5 \end{bmatrix}$$

• **Step 3**—$k = 2$ (not equal to 5). Do Step 2.
• **Step 2**—Using the same method, calculate D_3 and P:

$$D_3 = \begin{bmatrix} 0 & 2 & 3 & 4 & 7 \\ 2 & 0 & 1 & 2 & 5 \\ 3 & 5 & 0 & 1 & 10 \\ 1 & \infty & \infty & 0 & 2 \\ 6 & 8 & 3 & 4 & 0 \end{bmatrix}$$

$$P = \begin{bmatrix} 1 & 1 & 1 & 3 & 2 \\ 2 & 2 & 2 & 3 & 2 \\ 3 & 1 & 3 & 3 & 2 \\ 4 & 4 & 4 & 4 & 4 \\ 3 & 1 & 5 & 3 & 5 \end{bmatrix}$$

- **Step 3**—$k = 3$ (not equal to 5). Do Step 2.
- **Step 2**—Using the same method, calculate D_4 and P:

$$D_4 = \begin{bmatrix} 0 & 2 & 3 & 4 & 7 \\ 2 & 0 & 1 & 2 & 4 \\ 3 & 5 & 0 & 1 & 3 \\ 1 & \infty & \infty & 0 & 2 \\ 5 & 8 & 3 & 4 & 0 \end{bmatrix}$$

$$P = \begin{bmatrix} 1 & 1 & 1 & 3 & 2 \\ 2 & 2 & 2 & 3 & 4 \\ 3 & 1 & 3 & 3 & 4 \\ 4 & 4 & 4 & 4 & 4 \\ 4 & 1 & 5 & 3 & 5 \end{bmatrix}$$

- **Step 3**—$k = 4$ (not equal to 5). Do Step 2.
- **Step 2**—Using the same method, calculate D_5 and P:

$$D_5 = \begin{bmatrix} 0 & 2 & 3 & 4 & 7 \\ 2 & 0 & 1 & 2 & 4 \\ 3 & 5 & 0 & 1 & 3 \\ 1 & 3 & 5 & 0 & 2 \\ 5 & 8 & 3 & 4 & 0 \end{bmatrix}$$

$$P = \begin{bmatrix} 1 & 1 & 1 & 3 & 2 \\ 2 & 2 & 2 & 3 & 4 \\ 3 & 1 & 3 & 3 & 4 \\ 4 & 1 & 5 & 4 & 4 \\ 4 & 1 & 5 & 3 & 5 \end{bmatrix}$$

- **Step 3**—$k = 5$ (equal to 5). Stop.

The matrix D_5 contains the shortest distance for all possible pairs of nodes in the network. It can be used to estimate the cost of sending messages from node i to node j. The P matrix is useful because it provides the next node k that a message is sent to when it moves from node i on its way to node j.

Pollack's Algorithm

There may be occasions when you not only want to know the shortest path between two nodes, but you also want to know how much better the minimal path is than alternate paths. To determine how good the minimal path is, you have to know how long the second shortest path is.

A variety of methods have been developed for determining the second shortest path. Pollack's algorithm is one of the simplest, although not necessarily the most efficient. It is based on the fact that the second shortest path differs from the shortest path in at least one arc. The process is simple. First determine the shortest path and the arcs that make up the path using Dijkstra's algorithm. Then modify the network by eliminating one of the arcs in the shortest path. Finally, determine the shortest path in the modified network. To determine that the new path is indeed the second shortest path, the procedure must be repeated m times where m is the number of arcs in the original shortest path. A different arc is removed in each iteration. The formal algorithm is as follows:

Pollack's Algorithm for Second Shortest Paths

Step 1—Find the shortest path through the network. Number the arcs in the path 1 to m. Set $k = 1$, $q = \infty$.

Step 2—Set the length of arc k to ∞ temporarily. Find the shortest path through the modified network. If the length is less than q, set q equal to the length of the path.

Step 3—If $k = m$, stop. Otherwise, set $k = k + 1$ and repeat step 2.

Consider, for the final time, the network described in Figure 4-5. In an earlier example, the minimal distance from node 1 to node 5 was determined to be 6. The minimal path consists of four arcs, (1, 2), (2, 3), (3, 4), and (4, 5).

If arc (1, 2) is eliminated from the network, the minimal path length is still 6, but the path consists of three arcs, (1, 3), (3, 4), and (4, 5). Eliminating arc (2, 3) produces the identical result. If arc (3, 4) or (4, 5) is removed, the minimal path length is 7, passing along arcs (1, 2) and (2, 5). It appears that in this case, the minimal path is not that critical.

OPTIMAL FLOWS

A communications network consists of various forms of channels linking information transmitters and receivers. Each channel has a limited capacity for transmitting the information. In such a case, it is reasonable to ask what is the largest amount of information that can be transmitted during a fixed period of time. The limit may be a limit set by any portion of the network.

Besides the capacity associated with each channel, there is a cost associated with each transmission of a unit of information. This cost includes building and maintaining the various channels. One question that arises is, how can each user on the network be assured of having the ability to transmit and receive a fixed amount of information every day at a minimal cost. It also may be beneficial to know to what extent a disruption to a particular channel has on the overall network flow.

These problems are all related, as each deals with the flow of information over the network channels from transmitter to receiver. The process is easily portrayed as a network. The process can be studied under the general heading of flow algorithms.

The idea of flow is one of common sense, easily related to the communications problem. Information, generally measured in bits, moves over the network channels. Each channel has a maximal flow rate, generally expressed in bits per second. The processors generate the information that is passed over the channels. The communication network is conveniently related to a network of the previous discussions. Each arc (i, j) in the simplest form of the problem has a maximal flow rate $u(i, j)$ and an actual flow rate $x(i, j)$ which satisfies the inequality $0 \leq x(i, j) \leq u(i, j)$. The value of $u(i, j)$ is determined by the physical nature of the link.

When flows in arcs meet at nodes, it is desirable that no gain or loss in the flow occur at the node, except possibly at the ends of the network. This produces the constraint that the sum of flows into a node equal the sum of the flows out of the node. Using the terminology from above, $\sum x(i, j) = \sum x(j, k)$ for node j.

The only nodes in which the flow is not conserved are generally at the ends of the network. Sources are those nodes that generate flow. In a communications sense, sources are transmitters. Sinks are nodes that absorb flow. Sinks are the receivers or destinations of the information being passed over the network.

In the simplest case, a network has one source and one sink. These can be thought of as the s and t nodes from the earlier examples in the chapter. For this case, the problem to be considered is that of finding the largest flow rate from s to t, using the arcs of the networks, subject to the maximal flow rate associated with each arc and the conservation at each node except s and t.

Flow-Augmenting Chains

A flow-augmenting chain between a pair of nodes is a chain of arcs that connect the nodes and can be used to increase the flow from one node to another. In the case of flow in a network from source to sink, the chain will start at the source s and end at the sink t. Two kinds of arcs can exist in the chain, forward arcs and reverse arcs.

Forward arcs move information in the general direction from s to t and have spare capacity that can be used to increase the flow. Reverse arcs flow in the opposite sense. Network flow can be increased by reducing the flow rate in the reverse arcs. An example of this is a single communications channel between two points over which information can only flow in one direction at a time. The primary information path is from s to t, but acknowledgment information is sent from t to s periodically. If the accuracy of channel can be improved, there is a reduced need for acknowledgment. This increases the net flow rate.

The amount of change that can be achieved by use of a flow-augmenting chain is determined by the arc that is the closest to its limit on flow. For forward arcs, the limit is the upper bound. The amount of extra flow is the difference $u(i, j) - x(i, j)$. For reverse arcs, the limit is zero flow. The extra flow possible is limited by the amount of reduction possible, that is, the flow $x(i, j)$. For a flow-augmenting chain whose links are $(s, i_1), (i_1, i_2), \ldots, (i_r, i_{r+1}), \ldots, (i_q, t)$, the extra flow possible is found by determining the extra capacity in each arc. The capacity of the chain is the minimum over all arcs.

To demonstrate this concept, consider the flow-augmenting chains shown in Figure 4-11. Chain A consists of all forward arcs, Chain B consists of all reverse arcs, and Chain C contains a mixture. The possible extra flows in the three chains are 4, 2, and 3, respectively.

Maximal Flow Algorithm

The algorithm for finding the maximal flow in a network from a source to a sink consists of two parts. In the first part, a search is made to find a flow-augmenting chain linking the source and the sink. No special criteria is applied to the chain.

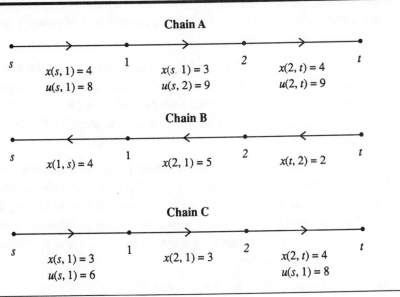

FIGURE 4-11 Flow-augmenting chains.

It just has to possess some unused flow capacity. The second step consists of making appropriate changes in the flows in each arc to increase the overall flow to a maximum. Once this is done, the first step is repeated, finding a new flow-augmenting chain. Then the flow is changed along this chain. The process continues in an iterative fashion until no flow-augmenting chains exist between the source and the sink.

The maximal flow algorithm described by Ford and Fulkerson uses a labeling scheme that assigns a two-part label to each node. The first component of the label indicates the source of the possible extra flow. The second part is the amount of extra flow that can be sent along the chain from s to the labeled node. The source of the extra flow is the previous node in the chain, either the head of a forward arc or the tail of a reverse arc. The formal statement of the algorithm is as follows:

Ford-Fulkerson Algorithm for Maximum Flow

Step 1—Give each arc a feasible flow, ensuring that the flow is conserved at each node other than s and t. This can be done by assigning a zero flow to each arc.

Step 2—Label node s with the label $(-, \infty)$ and ensure that no other node is labeled.

Step 3—Scan through the arcs until one (i, j) is found for which node i is labeled and node j is not and $x(i, j) < u(i, j)$ (a forward arc) or node j is labeled and node i is not and $x(i, j) > 0$ (a reverse arc). If no such arc exists, go to step 6.

Step 4—If step 3 identified a forward arc, label node j with the two-part label (a_j, b_j) where $a_j = i$, $b_j = \min[b_i, u(i, j) - x(i, j)]$. If step 3 identified a reverse arc, label node i with the two-part label (a_i, b_i) where $a_i = -i$, $b_i = \min[b_j, x(j, i)]$. If node t is now labeled, go to step 5. Otherwise, repeat step 3.

Step 5—A flow-augmenting chain has been found. Increase the flow in the chain by the amount b_t. If node t is labeled (l, t), increase the flow in the arc (l, t). If node t is labeled $(-l\ t)$, decrease the flow in the arc (t, l). Examine the label on node l and repeat the same procedure until the source is reached, always changing the flow by the amount b_t. When the source is reached, go to step 2.

Step 6—The optimal flow has been found. Stop.

Implementing this algorithm is not a simple task. To demonstrate the process, consider the simple example of the four-node, five-arc network shown in Figure 4-12. For this network, the maximal flow rates are defined as follows:

Arc ( )	$u(\ )$
(1, 2)	8
(2, 3)	5
(3, 4)	6
(1, 3)	3
(2, 4)	7

The algorithm produces the maximal possible flow from node 1 to node 4 in the following manner.

- **Step 1**—Assign zero flows to all arcs.
- **Step 2**—Label node 1 $(-, \infty)$.
- **Step 3**—Arc (1, 2) is a forward arc.
- **Step 4**—Label node 2 $(1, \min(\infty, 8-0)) = (1, 8)$.
- **Step 3**—Arc (2, 3) is a forward arc.
- **Step 4**—Label node 3 $(2, \min(8, 5-0)) = (2, 5)$.
- **Step 3**—Arc (3, 4) is a forward arc.
- **Step 4**—Label node 4 $(3, \min(5, 6-0)) = (3, 5)$. Sink node is now labeled.
- **Step 5**—Increase flow in the chain (1, 2), (2, 3), (3, 4) by 5. Now $x(3, 4) = x(2, 3) = x(1, 2) = 0 + 5 = 5$.
- **Step 2**—Label node 1 $(-, \infty)$.
- **Step 3**—Arc (1, 2) is a forward arc.
- **Step 4**—Label node 2 $(1, \min(\infty, 8-5)) = (1, 3)$.

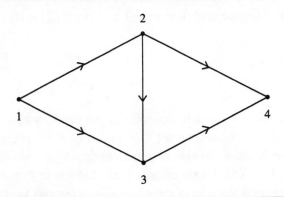

FIGURE 4-12 Network with flow.

- **Step 3**—Arc (1, 3) is a forward arc.
- **Step 4**—Label node 3 (1, min(∞, 3–0)) = (1, 3).
- **Step 3**—Arc (2, 4) is a forward arc.
- **Step 4**—Label node 4 (2, min(3, 7–0)) = (2, 3). Sink node is now labeled.
- **Step 5**—Increase the flow in the chain (1, 2) (2, 4) by 3. Now $x(2, 4) = 0 + 3 = 3, x(1, 2) = 5 + 3 = 8$.

- **Step 2**—Label node 1 (–, ∞).
- **Step 3**—Arc (1, 3) is a forward arc.
- **Step 4**—Label node 3 (1, min(∞, 3–0)) = (1, 3).
- **Step 3**—Arc (2, 3) is a reverse arc.
- **Step 4**—Label node 2 (–3, min(3, 5)) = (–3, 3).
- **Step 3**—Arc (3, 4) is a forward arc.
- **Step 4**—Label node 4 (3, min(3, 6–5)) = (3, 1). Sink node is now labeled.
- **Step 5**—Increase flow in the chain (1, 3), (3, 4) by 1. Now $x(3, 4) = 5 + 1 = 6, x(1, 3) = 0 + 1 = 1$.

- **Step 2**—Label node 1 (–, ∞).
- **Step 3**—Arc (1, 3) is a forward arc.
- **Step 4**—Label node 3 (1, min(∞, 3–1)) = (1, 2)
- **Step 3**—Arc (2, 3) is a reverse arc.
- **Step 4**—Label node 2 (–3, min(2, 2)) = (–3, 2).
- **Step 3**—Arc (2, 4) is a forward arc.
- **Step 4**—Label node 4 (2, min(2, 7–3)) = (2, 4). Sink node is now labeled.
- **Step 5**—Increase flow in the chain (1, 3), (2, 3) (2, 4) by 2. Now $x(2, 4) = 3 + 2 = 5, x(2, 3) = 5 – 2 = 3, x(1, 3) = 1 + 2 = 3$.

- **Step 2**—Label node 1 (–, ∞).
- **Step 3**—There are no arcs which meet the criteria.
- **Step 6**—Stop. The maximal flow from 1 to 4 is $x(1, 2) + x(1, 3) = 8 + 3 = 11$.

Cut-Sets

The concept of *cut-sets* is useful in determining the capacity of a network. A cut-set is a set of arcs that connects a set X of nodes of N to its complement. The source is in the set X while the sink is not. Denoting X' as the complement of X, the cut-set created by X is the set of arcs such that i is in X and j is in X'. The capacity of the cut-set is the sum of the capacities of the arcs in it.

As the flow passes from s to t, via various paths, each unit of flow must cross from X to X'. Therefore the capacity of the cut-set must be at least as large as the maximal flow from s to t through the network. Moreover, the value of the maximal flow is equal to the maximal capacity of all cut-sets in the network. This result is known as the *max flow-min cut theorem*.

Cut-sets can be used to determine the most critical arc in the network. This is the arc which, if removed, causes the greatest reduction the maximal flow. To determine the most critical arc, first rank the arcs in order of their flow. Then identify the arcs that appear in minimal cut-sets. If the arc with the largest flow is in the cut-set, it is the most critical arc. If this is not the case, arcs with flows larger than the arc with the largest flow in the cut-set must be deleted one at a time. One of these arcs will cause the greatest reduction.

SUMMARY

A graph $G(N, A)$ is a set of points N and a set A of ordered pairs of these points. The members of N are called *nodes*. The members of A are called *arcs*. Different properties are associated with the arcs, including the carrying capacity, length, and cost per unit flow. A *tree* is a connected graph that contains no cycles. The concept of a tree is used often in determining the optimal way to connect a group of nodes. A *spanning tree* is a tree that connects all nodes in a network or graph. A minimal spanning tree is one that minimizes some additive property of the arcs while connecting all nodes of the graph. The *Kruskal algorithm* and *Prim algorithm* determine the minimal spanning tree.

Networks are graphs that have one or more properties associated with each arc. Graphs and networks can be represented as matrices. These representations simplify some of the numerical operations when analyzing large networks. The two most common matrices are the *adjacency matrix* and the *incidence matrix*. If a property is associated with each arc, it is often represented in a form identical to the adjacency matrix.

Dijkstra's algorithm determines the shortest path between two arbitrary nodes on a network. *Ford's algorithm* determines the shortest path between a single node and all other nodes in the network and allows some arcs to have a negative cost or property value. *Floyd's algorithm* finds the shortest paths between all pairs of nodes. *Pollack's algorithm* determines the second shortest path.

The optimal flow through a network is determined by iteratively increasing the flow in *flow-augmenting chains* until no more such chains exist. This technique is called the *Ford-Fulkerson algorithm*. The maximal flow through a network is equal to the capacity of the *minimal cut-set*.

SUGGESTED READING

Wilson's *Introduction to Graph Theory* provides a general overview of graphs and the key definitions and concepts. Jensen and Barnes, in *Network Flow Programming*, and Smith, in *Network Optimisation Practices: A Computational Guide*, provide discussions of most of the algorithms presented in this chapter along with computer programs for implementing the algorithms. The basic concepts of network flows are discussed by Ford and Fulkerson in *Flows in Networks*. Bertsekas and Gallager relate many of the topics of graph and network theory to more specific data networks in their book, *Data Networks*.

5

QUEUEING THEORY

Reduced to its most basic structure, a data communications network consists of communication channels and communication processors. As shown in the previous chapter, it is easy to think of the processors as nodes and the channels as arcs or lines connecting the nodes, as shown in Figure 5-1. Messages pass over the channels, controlled by the processors. The processors encode and decode messages, route messages over different channels, and otherwise control the message traffic on the network.

As the messages move from node to node, queues begin to form at the different nodes as messages arrive and wait for service. A *queue* is a group of customers (in this case, messages) waiting for service. The primary factor in the time delay for a message to pass through the network is the length of the queues. The length of the queues depends on the statistics of the message arrival times and the service discipline of the processors.

Queueing theory plays a key role in the quantitative understanding of data communications networks. Queueing theory allows the concentration and

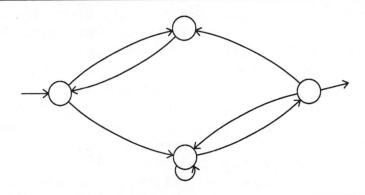

FIGURE 5-1 Arc-node network nepresentation.

buffering aspects of different network designs to be assessed before implementation. Queueing theory is also applied in a dynamic sense to provide optimum network performance by selecting message routing and controlling the network flow.

A data communications network is a complex system of servers and channels. The network is characterized by complex service disciplines between interconnected queues. The network has multiple resources, such as processors, buffers, switchers, and channels. Each processor is effectively a queueing network itself, with the central processor unit, memory, and data bus all being servers that process various requests for customers that arrive at different times.

Despite this complexity, a great deal of insight into the network performance can be gained by examining the properties of a single queue. A single queue consists of one or more identical servers and a line of awaiting customers. Requests come in over one channel and processed requests are passed out over another channel. A large segment of a data network can often be portrayed accurately as a single queue. Also, after single queue concepts are understood, the queues can be tied together to form a network of queues.

SINGLE QUEUES

A single queue consists of one or more servers and a series of customers who want service. Customers arrive at different times. If a server is free, the customer is processed immediately and sent on its way. If all servers are busy, a queue begins to form. As time goes on, the number of customers awaiting service will rise and, hopefully, fall. The queue is characterized by three quantities: the input process, the service mechanism, and the queue discipline.

The *input process* is the sequence of requests for service. The sequence is specified in terms of the length of time between consecutive arrivals. Generally, the specification takes the form of a probability distribution. The most common distributions are Poisson and deterministic.

The *service mechanism* describes how long the servers take to process each service request. The service time can be deterministic or possess some random behavior. In general, a queue can have several servers, each one performing an identical service for the next awaiting customer.

The *queue discipline* describes the disposition of the customers in line. The simplest form is when no queue forms at all. If the customer requests service and all servers are busy, the customer goes away. What happens more often is that the queue begins to form if the servers are busy. There are several ways in which the waiting customers are chosen for service. The most common ones are *first in, first out* (FIFO), *first in, last out* (FILO), and *first in, random out* (FIRO). It is also possible to assign different priorities to different classes of customers. Another factor that describes the queue discipline is the maximum length of the queue, or the maximum number of customers that are allowed to wait in line. The simplest case is when the maximum length is infinite.

Little's Formula

One of the basic formulas of queueing theory is *Little's formula*. It is stated in many ways, but its meaning is straightforward and somewhat intuitive. The power of the formula is that it holds regardless of the input process, service mechanism, or queue discipline. The formula is as follows.

> Let λ equal the average arrival rate of customers over a period of time. Let T equal the average amount of time required to service each customer. Then N, the average number of customers in the system, is equal to the product of λ and T or
>
> $$N = \lambda T$$

To derive the formula, consider a simple single server system. Define $N(t)$ as the number of customers in the system at time t. The number of customers is the number of customers lined up in the queue plus the one in the server. Let a_i be the time of arrival of the ith customer and $A(t)$ be the number of customers who arrive before time t. Assume $A(0) = 0$. Let d_i be the time of departure of the ith customer and $D(t)$ be the number of customers who have departed (received service) before time t.

Therefore, $N(t) = A(t) - D(t)$. Furthermore, the total time that the ith customer is in the system is $T_i = d_i - a_i$. The waiting time, the time spent in the queue before getting service, is $W_i = T_i - S_i$, where S_i is the service time for the ith customer.

Now consider two times a and b. Select a and b such that $a < b$ and $N(a) = N(b) = 0$. Furthermore, at times just greater than a and b, defined as $a+$ and $b+$, $N(a+) = N(b+) = 1$. This process is shown in Figure 5-2. The average number of customers in the system over the interval $[a, b]$ is

$$N = \int_a^b N(t)\, dt\, (b - a)$$

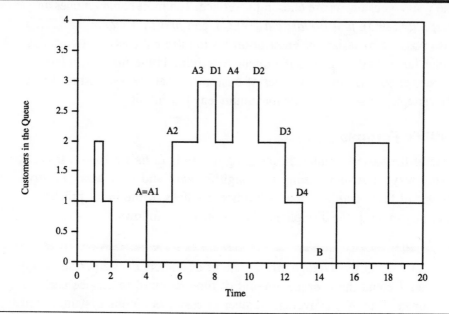

FIGURE 5-2   Demonstration of Little's formula process.

Over the interval $[a, b]$, k customers arrive at times specified by

$$a = a_{i1} < a_{i2} < \cdots < a_{ik} < b$$

Because $N(a) = N(b) = 0$, all customers who arrive in the interval also must depart in the interval. So for every a_{ij}, there is a corresponding $d_{ij} \le b$. Therefore, the average time each customer spends in the queue and being serviced is

$$T = \sum_{i=1}^{k} (d_{ij} - a_{ij})/k$$

Because k customers arrive in the interval, the average arrival rate $\lambda(a, b)$ is equal to $k/(b - a)$. Therefore

$$\lambda(a, b)\, T = \sum_{i=1}^{k} (d_{ij} - a_{ij})/(b - a) = N$$

Notice that this formula is derived without any assumptions as to the probability distributions associated with the arrival process or the service mechanism. The only assumptions are that two times a and b exist where $N(t) = 0$.

Kendall Notation

Because a queue is specified by its arrival process, service mechanism, and queue discipline, a notation was developed to succinctly define a queue. The notation is called the *Kendall notation*. It is expressed as a series of letters separated by slashes ("/")

$$A/B/C/K/m/z$$

where the letters represent

- A   Arrival process
- B   Service process
- C   Number of servers. The simplest case is a single server. When the queue has multiple servers, the servers perform identical service operations.
- K   Maximum capacity. This is the maximum number of customers that are allowed to wait in queue for service. The simplest case is when $K = \infty$. When $K = \infty$, it is generally omitted from the notation.
- m   Population of customers. The simplest case is when $m = \infty$. If m is finite, the arrival rate may decrease as a large percentage of customers join the queue. As in the case of K, when $m = \infty$, it is generally omitted from the notation.
- z   Service discipline. The principle service disciplines are FIFO, FILO, and FIRO. If the z is omitted, FIFO is assumed.

The letters A and B assume specific letters for the different probability distributions. The letters are:

- GI General independent arrival times or processing times. The arrival times and service times can be any distribution, but all arrival times and service times are independent.
- G   General arrival times or processing times. The arrival times and service times can be any distribution, but all arrival times and service times are not necessarily independent.
- H_k Hyperexponential distribution of order k.
- E_k Erlang distribution of order k.
- M   Poisson arrival times or exponential service times.
- D   Constant (deterministic) arrival times or service times.

Some of the more common queues are $M/M/1$ (Poisson arrival times, exponential service times, single server, infinite queue length, infinite number of customers, and FIFO queue discipline), $M/M/n$ (Poisson arrival times, exponential service times, n servers, infinite queue length, infinite number of customers, and FIFO queue discipline), and $M/GI/1$ (Poisson arrival times, general independent service times, single server, infinite queue length, infinite number of customers, and FIFO queue discipline).

M/M/1 Queue

The $M/M/1$ queue is the simplest queue to analyze. Because of this, many of the developments in queueing theory were originally developed for a $M/M/1$ queue and later extended to more general results. Despite its simplicity, the $M/M/1$ queue provides an accurate representation of many of the processes associated with data communications.

As its name implies, the $M/M/1$ queue assumes that customers arrive at a Poisson distributed rate. When there are n customers in the queue (counting equally the customer being served), the arrival process, as stated above, is Poisson with parameter λ_n. In most cases $\lambda_n = \lambda$, a constant rate for the queue. The Poisson is the most common description of the arrival process in queueing theory.

Data communications traffic is often modeled as a Poisson process. One advantage of this approach is that the Poisson distribution is described completely by the average arrival rate, λ. If you want to simulate an arrival process with a Poisson distribution, you only need to measure the average arrival rate on the actual network to portray the queue arrival process.

In data communications, the server is somewhat different from the traditional queueing theory server. In data communications, the server is often a fixed capacity outgoing line that continually transmits C data units per unit time (if messages are available to be transmitted). The statistical variation in the service time is due to variations in message length.

Exponential service time is the simplest queueing theory assumption. The service time is exponentially distributed with rate μ_n. Part of the simplicity of the exponential distribution derives from its "memoryless" property. It is possible to start the service again (or equivalently, continue it) when a customer with a new parameter μ_{n+1} enters the queue. More general service time distributions require that the amount of service time already provided be accounted for.

Although the exponential distribution is continuous while messages have discrete lengths, the exponential distribution provides quick, simple results when data communications networks are designed and analyzed. It readily adapts to the concept of variable message lengths accounting for varying service times. If the average message length is $1/\mu$ data units per message, the probability density function is, assuming $\mu(n) = \mu$,

$$f(r) = \mu e^{-\mu r}$$

If the outgoing channel capacity is C, each message takes r/C units of time to transmit. Therefore, the *service time distribution* becomes

$$f(t) = \mu C e^{-\mu C t}$$

The average time to transmit a message is $1/\mu C$. This quantity, called the average service time, is often denoted as τ.

To determine the performance of a network portrayed as an $M/M/1$ queue, you need to find the probability $p_n(t)$ that n messages are present in the buffer at time t. This provides a state description that can be used to determine various statistical parameters, such as average buffer occupancy, probability of exceeding a given occupancy level, and average delay time. If the queue does not grow without bound, as $t \rightarrow \infty$, a steady-state description of the queue can be determined.

The $M/M/1$ queue is readily portrayed as a birth-death Markov process. This is a Markov process in which only two transitions are possible. The process can increase by 1 (a birth) or decrease by 1 (a death). In the $M/M/1$ queue, the number of customers in the queue is a birth-death process. A birth is the addition of a customer to the queue. A death is the completion of service for a customer, resulting in the decrease of the queue.

To determine $p_n(t)$, you need to find the transition matrix P associated with the Markov process. Let n be the number of messages in the buffer and E_n be the state associated with n. If λ_n is the message arrival rate, then the rate of transition from state E_n to E_{n+1} is λ_n. If μ_n is the service rate, the rate of transition from state E_n to E_{n-1} is μ_n. Similarly, the rate of transition from E_n to E_n is $-\lambda_n - \mu_n$. Therefore P is

$$P = \begin{bmatrix} -\lambda_0 & \lambda_0 & 0 & 0 & 0 \\ \mu_1 & -\lambda_1 - \mu_1 & \lambda_1 & 0 & 0 \\ 0 & \mu_2 & -\lambda_2 - \mu_2 & \lambda_2 & 0 \\ & & \cdot & \cdot & \cdot \\ 0 & 0 & & \cdot & \cdot \end{bmatrix}$$

After you have the transition matrix, you can find the stationary solution (if one exists) by considering the solution $p = (p_0, p_1, \dots)$ of the system $pP = 0$ and $p1 = 1$. This results in the solution that

$$p_n = p_0 (\lambda_0 \lambda_1 \cdots \lambda_{n-1})/(\mu_1 \mu_2 \cdots \mu_n)$$

p_0 is defined by the condition that the sum of the probabilities equal one, or

$$p_0 [1 + \Sigma (\lambda_0 \lambda_1 \cdots \lambda_{n-1})/(\mu_1 \mu_2 \cdots \mu_n)] = 1$$

Notice that if the sum of the probabilities does not equal one, there is no statistical equilibrium and the queue will grow without bound. In other words, the ergodicity condition of the Markov process is

$$1 + \Sigma (\lambda_0 \lambda_1 \cdots \lambda_{n-1})/(\mu_1 \mu_2 \cdots \mu_n) < \infty$$

When this condition is met, the transition probabilities become

$$p_0 = 1/[1 + \Sigma (\lambda/\mu)^n] = 1 - \lambda/\mu$$
$$p_n = p_0 (\lambda/\mu)^n = (1 - \lambda/\mu)(\lambda/\mu)^n$$

The quantity λ/μ appears often in the analysis of data communications networks. It is a measure of the demand on the system. It is given various names, including *Erlang* or *traffic intensity*. Because the probability that the queue is empty p_0, the probability that the queue is not empty is $1 - p_0 = \rho$. It is generally denoted by the symbol $\rho = \lambda/\mu$. Because the probability that the queue is empty is p_0, the probability that the queue is not empty is $1 - p_0 = \rho$. The formula for p_n can be expressed in terms of ρ as

$$p_n = (1 - \rho) \rho^n$$

It is apparent from the derived value for p_n that a necessary condition for a steady-state queue (and an ergodic Markov process) is that $\rho < 1$. This agrees with the intuitive notion that the messages have to be processed at a faster rate, on average, than they arrive. Otherwise, the length of the queue becomes infinitely long. Also, as ρ gets large, the probability of a longer queue increases. The probability that the queue is not empty is $1 - p_0 = \rho$. A portion of the steady state queue in the arc-node format is shown in Figure 5-3.

The average size of the queue can be readily determined as

$$E(n) = \Sigma n p_n = \rho/(1 - \rho)$$

The average queue occupancy increases without bound as ρ approaches 1, as shown in Figure 5-4.

The average time delay is related to the queue occupancy. If the average message takes τ units of time to send, the time from when a messages enters a

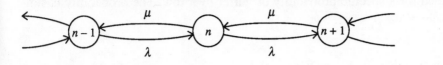

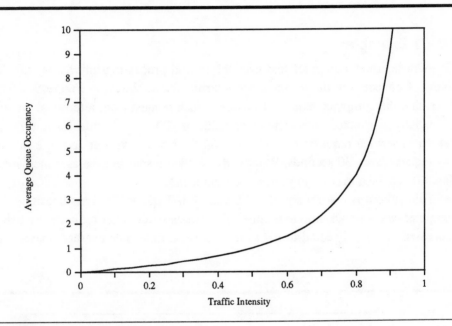

FIGURE 5-3 Steady-state queue.

FIGURE 5-4 Average queue occupancy.

queue is equal to the time it takes for it to be transmitted plus the time for all messages ahead of it in the queue to be transmitted. Letting T_i be the time delay and n_i be the number of messages in the queue when the ith message arrives,

$$T_i = \tau + n_i \, \tau = \tau (n_i + 1)$$

From the rules of probability,

$$E(T) = \tau [E(N) + 1] = \tau/(1 - \rho)$$

This can also be expressed as $E(T) \, \lambda = E(N)$, which is Little's formula.

Another useful quantity is the probability that the length of the queue exceeds a specified number, N. This quantity is useful in determining the buffer size needed for a specific probability of buffer overflow. The probability is simply the sum of the p_i's for $i > n$.

$$P(n > N) = \sum_{n=N+1}^{\infty} p_n = (1 - \rho) \sum_{n=N+1}^{\infty} \rho^n = \rho^{N+1}$$

Figure 5-5 shows these probabilities graphically for different values of ρ and N.

M/M/1 Example

Consider a simple computer that uses the central processing unit as its only resource. Connected to the terminal are n terminals, as shown in Figure 5-6. The times that the computer requires to process each request from a terminal are exponentially distributed with an average value of 200 milliseconds. Each terminal generates service requests that are Poisson distributed with an average rate of one request every 30 seconds. What is the service response time as n increases? Should there be a maximum number of terminals?

This system is readily simulated by an M/M/1 queue. This assumes that the computer can store an infinite number of requests while other requests are being processed. $\tau = 1/\mu$ is equal to the average service time. The average arrival rate

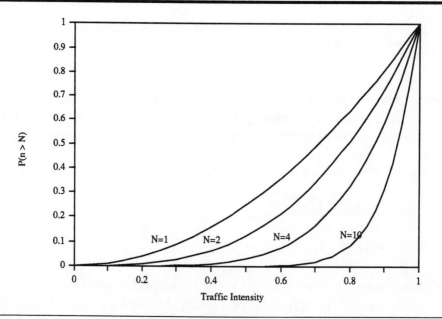

FIGURE 5-5   Probability of exceeding a specified buffer size.

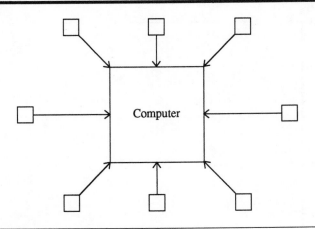

FIGURE 5-6 Network of computer terminals.

is $n\lambda$ because the requests from the terminals can be combined into one large service requester. Therefore, ρ, equal to the product of the arrival rate and the service time, is

$$\rho = n\lambda\tau = n(0.05)(0.200) = 0.01n$$

The first thing to notice is that if the number of terminals exceeds 100, ρ becomes greater than one, and the queue will become infinitely long. Therefore the maximum number of terminals allowed is 100. With 100 terminals, the average response time will still approach infinity.

The average number of requests in the queue is simply $\rho/(1 - \rho)$ or $0.01n/(1 - 0.01n)$. The behavior is shown in Figure 5-7 on the following page. Notice that as n approaches 100, the queue is very long. The net result is that every terminal is waiting on a service request. The average response time is directly related to the length of the queue. For the assumed queue, the average response time is

$$E(T) = \tau/(1 - \rho) = 0.200/(1 - 0.01n)$$

Figure 5-8 on the following page demonstrates the behavior of the response time as the number of terminals is increased. Notice the similarity between the average queue size and the average response time. The curves are identical except for a scalar constant. As noted above, as n approaches 100, the response time gets very long. If the number of terminals stays below 80, however, the average response time is less than one second.

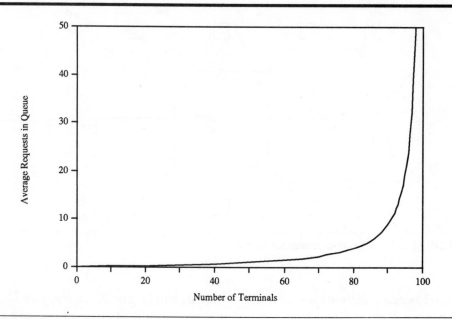

FIGURE 5-7   Average queue size.

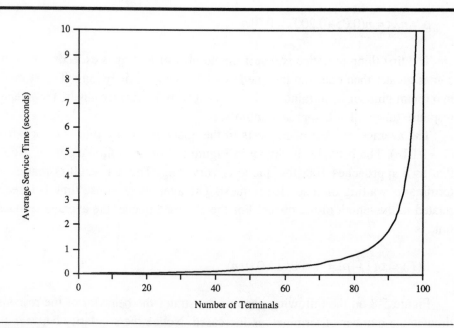

FIGURE 5-8   Average response time.

When the system was designed, an average response time of one second was the maximum allowable. But as the number of terminals climbs past 80, achieving this factor is becoming impossible. The computer manufacturer, however, has just announced an upgrade that increases the performance of the computer by 20 percent. Assuming that this provides a proportional reduction in the average service time, will this allow you to connect more terminals and still maintain the one-second delay criteria?

A 20-percent performance improvement implies that τ is reduced from 200 milliseconds to 160 milliseconds. Therefore ρ is $0.008n$. Recall that

$$E(T) = \tau/(1 - \rho) = 0.160/(1 - 0.008n) = 1$$

Solving for n yields the result that, if you upgrade the computer, you can accommodate 105 terminals and still maintain the one-second average delay.

M/M/1/K Queue

The previous derivation of the steady-state probability of state occupancy assumed an infinitely large buffer (i. e., an $M/M/1/\infty$ queue), but it did not actually use the fact. The solution for the finite buffer case (an $M/M/1/K$ queue) is similar. The transition matrix P is identical, except that it is now finite, ending with the state E_K. The last row (K^{th} row) in the matrix is $[0\ 0 \cdots 0\ \mu_K - \mu_K]$.

Assuming that $\lambda_0 = \lambda_1 = \cdots = \lambda$, $\mu_1 = \mu_2 = \cdots = \mu$, and $\lambda/\mu = \rho$, the solution for the transition probabilities yields the same result for p_n for $n \le k$, $p_n = p_0\, \rho^n$. For $n > k$, $p_n = 0$. The expression for p_0, however, is changed slightly. The summation is now over the values of n from 0 to K, rather than $n = 0$ to ∞. Therefore,

$$\sum_{n=0}^{K} p_n = 1 = p_0 \sum_{n=0}^{K} \rho^n = p_0\, [(1 - \rho^{K+1})/(1 - \rho)]$$

and $p_0 = (1 - \rho)/(1 - \rho^{K+1})$. Notice as $K \to \infty$, this reduces to the $M/M/1$ queue.

Because the queue has a finite length, there is a finite probability that the buffer is filled when a message arrives and that messages are turned away or blocked from entering the queue. This probability is often referred to as the *blocking probability*, P_B. For the $M/M/1/K$ queue, P_B is simply the probability that there are N messages in the buffer or

$$P_B = p_N = (1 - \rho)\rho^N/(1 - \rho^{N+1})$$

λP_B of the messages are blocked from entering the queue and turned away. The net arrival rate is $\lambda(1 - P_B)$. The blocking probability is sometimes referred to as the Erlang loss value for the queue. Different values for P_B as a function of ρ, the traffic intensity, and N are shown in Figure 5-9 on the following page.

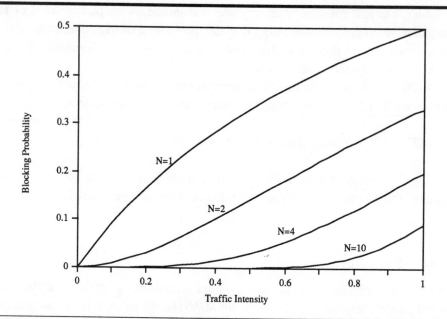

FIGURE 5-9   *M/M/1/N* blocking probabilities.

M/M/1/K Example

Consider again the simple computer that uses the central processing unit as its only resource. Connected to the terminal are *n* terminals. The processing times are exponentially distributed with an average value of 200 milliseconds. Each terminal generates service requests that are Poisson distributed with an average rate of one request every 30 seconds. But now the computer is assumed to have a limited buffer size, *K*. Once *K* requests are in the queue, additional requests are blocked until a request leaves the queue. What percentage of requests are blocked? What is the service response time as different buffer sizes? What is the benefit of increasing the buffer size? Is there a benefit to reducing the buffer size?

This process is now readily simulated by an *M/M/1/K* queue. This assumes that the computer can store *K* requests while other requests are being processed. ρ, equal to the product of the arrival rate and the service time, is still

$$\rho = n\lambda\tau = n(0.05)(0.200) = 0.01n$$

Recall from the previous example that when $n = 80$, the average queue size is 4. If you let *K* equal 5, you might expect that the percentage of requests blocked will be low. The system is now an *M/M/1/5* queue. For 80 terminals,

$\rho = 0.8$. The blocking probability is, as shown earlier, the transition probability for 5. The result is

$$p_5 = (1 - 0.8)0.8^5/(1 - 0.8^{5+1}) = 0.0888$$

Almost 10 percent of the requests are blocked. If the buffer is increased to store 10 requests, the probability of a busy signal falls to 0.0235. Expanding the buffer to 20 requests lowers the probability to 0.0023.

To compensate for blocking a percentage of the requests, a finite queue size provides two benefits. First, it reduces the hardware costs, because less equipment is required to store the queued requests. Second, the average queue size is reduced, resulting in a smaller average delay time. Table 5-1 summarizes the results for a finite queue size. The corresponding results from an infinite queue ($M/M/1$) are shown for comparison.

TABLE 5-1 $M/M/1/K$ queue statistics.

Queue Size	P_B	$E(N)$	$E(T)$
5	0.088	1.868	0.574
10	0.023	2.966	0.793
20	0.002	3.804	0.961
∞	0.000	4.000	1.000

M/M/C Queue

Another useful extension of the $M/M/1$ single server queue is the multiple server queue, the $M/M/C$. A typical $M/M/C$ queue is a simple communications network consisting of C lines between two concentrators. As calls come into the concentrators, they are assigned to each available line until all lines are being used. Then the queue starts. As soon as a line becomes free, the longest waiting call is assigned to it.

The transition probabilities are determined in a similar manner to the $M/M/1$ case. Again let n be the number of messages in the buffer and E_n be the state associated with n. If λ is the message arrival rate, then the rate of transition from state E_n to E_{n+1} is still λ. The rate of transition from state E_n to E_{n-1}, however, changes slightly. If $\tau = 1/\mu$ is the service time, the rate of transition state E_n to E_{n-1} is $n\mu$ for $n \leq C$. For $n > C$, the rate is $C\mu$. The n term accounts for the fact that if the state is E_n, any of the n occupied lines can become free and result in a system in state E_{n-1}.

The stationary solution is only achievable if $\lambda/C\mu < 1$. If this is the case,

$$p_0 = \left[\sum_{k=0}^{C-1} (\rho)^k/k! + \sum_{k=C}^{\infty} (\rho/C)^k \right]^{-1}$$

and

$$p_n = \begin{cases} p_0 \rho^n/n! & n \le C \\ p_0 \rho^n/C! \; C^{n-C} & n > C \end{cases}$$

The second summation in the p_0 formula converges to $\rho^C/(C-1)!(C-\rho)$. The expected queue occupancy is

$$E(N) = [\rho^{C+1}/(C-1)!(C-\rho)^2] \, p_0 + \rho$$

A more typical case assumes a zero-length queue, a $M/M/C/C$ queue. The queue can only contain as many calls as it has servers (or communication lines). You get a busy signal if all lines are occupied. The transition probabilities again are determined in a similar manner but altered slightly, because p_n is equal to 0 for $n > C$. Because of this, the transition probabilities have a simpler form. The results are

$$p_0 = \sum_{k=0}^{C} [(\rho)^k/k!]^{-1}$$

and

$$p_n = \begin{cases} p_0 \rho^n/n! & n \le C \\ 0 & n > C \end{cases}$$

Because the queue is defined as being of zero length, the average queue occupancy is identically less than one. The average time delay is simply the average service time. The blocking probability is p_n when $n = C$. Figure 5-10 illustrates the behavior of the blocking probability as a function of ρ, the traffic intensity. C in this case is the number of servers. Notice that for $C = 1$ (a single server), the result is identical to that shown in Figure 5-9. As the number of servers are increased, however, the blocking probability falls off much more rapidly than if the incoming messages were allowed to form a queue.

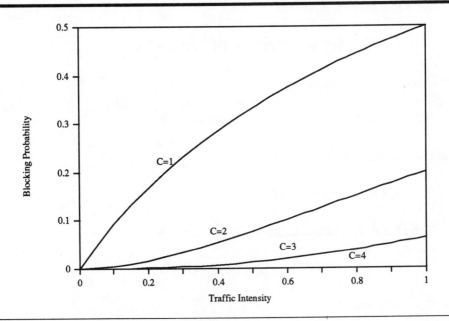

FIGURE 5-10 *M/M/C/1* blocking probabilities.

The quantity $\rho = \lambda/\mu = \lambda\tau$ is also referred to as the *offered load* on the queue. The quantity ρ' is referred to as the *carried load*. The carried load is the average number of busy servers and is equal to $\rho(1 - P_B)$. The *utilization factor* is equal to the carried loaded divided by the number of servers, $\rho(1 - P_B)/C$.

M/M/C Example

Consider again the computer system with a central processor serving n terminals. The average service time is still 200 milliseconds, and each terminal still generates a request every 30 seconds on average. In the previous example, you saw that with $n = 80$, the average queue size was 4 and the average delay was one second. The number of terminals has recently gone to 90, and users are complaining because the average service time is now 20 seconds.

You decide to add a second identical central processor. How does this addition affect the average queue size? How much is the average delay time reduced? How many terminals can be added to the system while still maintaining a one-second average delay time?

The system is now modelled by an *M/M/2* queue. The traffic intensity is

$$\rho = n\lambda\tau = 90(0.05)(0.200) = 0.9$$

With two servers, p_0 is

$$p_0 = [1 + 0.9 + (0.9^2)/(2 - 1)!(2 - 0.9)]^{-1} = 0.3793,$$

the expected queue size is,

$$E(N) = p_0\, 0.9^3/[(2 - 1)!(2 - 0.9)^2] + 0.9 = 1.1285,$$

and the average delay time is

$$E(T) = 0.2[E(N) + 1] = 0.4257$$

If the number of terminals grows to 160, $\rho = 1.6$, p_0 is

$$p_0 = [1 + 1.6 + (1.6^2)/(2 - 1)!(2 - 1.6)]^{-1} = 0.1111,$$

the expected queue size is,

$$E(N) = p_0\, 1.6^3/[(2 - 1)!(2 - 1.6)^2] + 1.6 = 4.4444,$$

and the average delay time is

$$E(T) = 0.2[E(N) + 1] = 1.0889$$

This performance is not quite as good as two central processors serving two independent groups of 80 terminals each.

The previous two examples assumed that the central processor possesses an infinite queue to store requests from the terminals until it processes them. What if the processors have no capability to store requests? If the number of terminals is 160, how many servers are needed to keep the percentage of blocked requests less than two percent?

You now have an $M/M/2/2$ queue. If the number of terminals is 160, ρ is 1.6,

$$p_0 = [1 + 1.6 + 1.6^2/2!]^{-1} = 0.2577$$
$$p_B = p_2 = p_0(1.6^2/2!) = 0.3299$$

The carried load is $\rho' = (1.6)(1 - 0.3299) = 1.0722$. The utilization factor is equal to 0.5361. This illustrates what is seemingly a paradox. Although each server is used, on average, slightly more than 50 percent of the time, almost one-third of all service requests are blocked because all servers are busy.

If you increase the number of available lines to five, you have an $M/M/5/5$ queue. ρ is still 1.6.

$$p_0 = [1 + 1.6 + 1.6^2/2! + 1.6^3/3! + 1.6^4/4! + 1.6^5/5! \,]^{-1} = 0.3846$$
$$p_B = p_5 = p_0(1.6^5/5!) = 0.0177$$

The carried load is $\rho' = (1.6)(1 - 0.0177) = 1.5716$. The utilization factor is equal to 0.3143. You have now greatly reduced the blocking probability, but at the cost of adding three additional servers. Also, each server is used, on average, only one-third of the time.

M/G/1 Queue

The assumption of an exponential distribution of service times (or message lengths), although a good approximation to many data communications systems, cannot be applied to all systems. There are systems in which the message lengths are not exponentially distributed. One obvious example is when all messages are of a fixed length, as in a packet-switched network. Because all messages are the same length, the processing times and transmission times for all messages are deterministic.

If you assume that the service requests continue to arrive at a Poisson distributed rate, it turns out that a very powerful expression can be derived for the average number of customers in the queue and the average waiting time. The expression, called the *Pollaczek-Khinchine formula*, holds for any distribution of service times as long as the variance of the service times is finite.

Analysis of cases involving a general message length, an $M/G/1$ queue, is approached differently from an $M/M/1$ queue. Because the memoryless property of the exponential distribution no longer holds, the future of the process depends not only on the present size of the queue, but also on the amount of time already spent serving the customer in the queue at a specific instant. This difficulty can be eliminated, however, if you consider only the future size of the queue from time T of departure onward.

As in the $M/M/1$ case, N is an arrival process with a Poisson rate of λ. The service times are independent of each other and of the arrival process and have an unspecified distribution function. But rather than focusing on the queue size as before, let X_n be the number of customers in the system just after the instant of the nth departure. Assume, for simplicity, that the time origin is also an instant of departure. With these assumptions, X is a Markov chain.

Not only is X a Markov chain, its behavior depends on a single parameter, the traffic intensity ρ. ρ is defined essentially as before as the product of expected arrival rate and the expected waiting time, $\lambda\tau$. As before, if $\rho > 1$, the server cannot keep up with the arrivals and the queue becomes infinitely long. If $\rho \leq 1$, the server can clear its work load. If $\rho = 1$, however, the expected time to clear the work load is infinite.

The derivation of the Pollaczek-Khinchine formula is generally developed using moment generating functions. These are transforms of probability distributions. The resulting formula, however, is much simpler than its derivation. For this reason, it is simply stated.

If a $M/G/1$ queueing process exists with a Poisson arrival rate with parameter λ and a service time distribution with mean service time τ and a service time variance of σ^2, the expected number of customers in the queue is

$$E(N) = (1/2(1 - \rho)[\sigma^2 + \rho(1 - \rho)]$$

where $\rho = \lambda\tau$.

An alternate expression for the expected number of customers in the queue is

$$E(N) = [1/(1 - \rho)][\rho - (\rho^2/2)(1 - \sigma^2/\tau^2)]$$

This latter formulation demonstrates clearly that the average number of customers in the queue is related directly to the traffic intensity factor ρ, the average service time τ, and the variance of the service time σ^2.

Utilizing Little's formula, the average time in the queue is

$$E(T) = 1/\lambda\, E(N) = [\tau/(1 - \rho)][1 - (\rho/2)(1 - \sigma^2/\tau^2)]$$

If you assume that the service time distribution is exponential, the variance of the service time σ^2 is equal to τ^2. The expected number of customers in the queue is $\rho/(1 - \rho)$, and the average time in the queue is $\tau/(1 - \rho)$. These results are, as expected, the same as previously determined for the $M/M/1$ queue.

If the service time distribution is such that all service times are constant (as in the case of messages of equal lengths), σ^2 is equal to 0. The expected number of customers in the queue is now $[1/(1 - \rho)][\rho - (\rho^2/2)]$. The average time in queue is $[\tau/(1 - \rho)][1 - (\rho/2)]$. Both the mean queue size and the service time are reduced.

In general, the ratio σ^2/τ^2 provides a good indication of the behavior of a queue. If $\sigma^2/\tau^2 < 1$, the expected length of and average time in the $M/G/1$ queue is less than for a $M/M/1$ queue. When $\sigma^2/\tau^2 > 1$, the average length and time increase. If $\sigma^2/\tau^2 = 1$, the average length and time are the same as the $M/M/1$ queue. This relationship is depicted in Figure 5-11. R denotes the value of σ^2/τ^2. $R = 0$ is a $M/D/1$ queue, $R = 1$ is a $M/M/1$ queue, and $R = 4$ is a $M/G/1$ queue where the variance of the service time is such that $\sigma^2/\tau^2 = 4$.

Another useful quantity that can be derived from the Pollaczek-Khinchine formula is the average waiting time, $E(W)$. The waiting time is simply the average time in the queue less the service time, or

$$E(W) = E(T) - 1/\mu$$

Substituting the result for $E(T)$ yields

$$E(W) = (\lambda/2)[(\sigma^2 + (1/\mu)^2]/(1 - \rho)$$

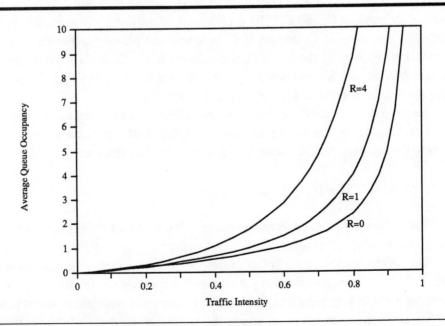

FIGURE 5-11   Average queue size for $M/G/1$ queue.

Because of the laws of probability, the quantity $\sigma^2 + (1/\mu)^2$ is equal to $E(\tau^2)$ where τ is the service time. Therefore, the expressions for the expected waiting time becomes

$$E(W) = (\lambda/2)E(\tau^2)/(1 - \rho)$$

Queues with Priority

Until now, all customers have been assumed to be equal in the eyes of the server. This assumption does not accurately reflect real-world data communications systems. In the real world, different classes of messages often exist. Different classes of messages have different priorities. Messages with higher priority are recognized as such by the server and allowed to move to the front of the queue as soon as they enter. Messages with lower priorities are bumped back.

Different classes of messages may be assigned to different users in a communications network. The systems administrator often has a priority that allows him to broadcast a message to all users, preempting all other messages in the queue. Short acknowledgment messages are often assigned a higher priority, because they enable the transmitting end to begin processing the next segment of a message. Messages that are longer than normal are often assigned a low priority to prevent them from tying up a network.

The simplest queue with priority is an $M/M/1$ queue with two classes of customers, denoted as C_1 and C_2. The proportions of customers in class are represented by α and $1 - \alpha$. Customers in C_1 have absolute priority in that they are not affected in any way by the lower class customers in C_2. Each class has a Poisson arrival rate (λ_1 and λ_2) and an exponential service time (τ_1 and τ_2). The arrival rate can also be expressed as $\lambda_1 = \lambda\alpha$ and $\lambda_2 = \lambda(1 - \alpha)$.

Because the first-class customers are not affected in any way by the second-class customers, the transition probabilities for the first-class customers are identical to the standard $M/M/1$ queue. The transition probabilities are:

$$p_1(n) = (\lambda_1\tau_1)^n[1 - (\lambda_1\tau_1)^n] = \rho_1^n(1 - \rho_1^n)$$

The values from the expected length of the queue and the expected time in the queue are also identical.

The results for the second-class customers are somewhat different. Because the service times are exponentially distributed, resuming service for the C_2 customers after it is interrupted to service a C_1 customer is equivalent to restarting service altogether. Let n_1 and n_2 denote the number of each class in the queue at any instant in time. There are four possible cases: (1) $n_1 > 0$, $n_2 > 0$; (2) $n_1 = 0$, $n_2 > 0$; (3) $n_1 > 0$, $n_2 = 0$; and (4) $n_1 = 0$, $n_2 = 0$.

Letting $p(n_1, n_2)$ denote the probability of having n_1 class C_1 customers and n_2 class C_2 customers, the equilibrium equation for each case is as follows:

Case 1: $(\lambda_1 + \lambda_2 + \mu_1)p(n_1, n_2) = \lambda_1 p(n_1 - 1, n_2) + \mu_1 p(n_1 + 1, n_2) +$
$\qquad \lambda_2 p(n_1, n_2 - 1)$
Case 2: $(\lambda_1 + \lambda_2 + \mu_1)p(n_1, 0) = \lambda_1 p(n_1 - 1, 0) + \mu_1 p(n_1 + 1, 0)$
Case 3: $(\lambda_1 + \lambda_2 + \mu_2)p(0, n_2) = \mu_1 p(1, n_2) + \lambda_2 p(0, n_2 - 1) + \mu_2 p(0, n_2 + 1)$
Case 4: $(\lambda_1 + \lambda_2)p(0, 0) = \mu_1 p(1, 0) + \mu_2 p(0, 1)$

Finding the equilibrium solution from this series of equations is tedious and is omitted from this discussion. The stability condition is that $\rho_1 + \rho_2 < 1$. The expected numbers of each class of customer in the queue are:

$E[N_1] = \rho_1/(1 - \rho_1)$
$E[N_2] = [\rho_2 + E(N_1)\rho_2]/(1 - \rho_1 - \rho_2) = [\rho_2/(1 - \rho_1)]/(1 - \rho_1 - \rho_2)$

To demonstrate the effects of this simple two-class system, let $\rho = \lambda/\mu$, $\lambda_1 = \alpha\lambda$, $\lambda_2 = (1 - \alpha)\lambda$, and $\mu = \mu_1 = \mu_2$. Then $\rho_1 = \alpha\rho$ and $\rho_2 = (1 - \alpha)\rho$. The expected values of each class become

$E[N_1] = \alpha\rho/(1 - \alpha\rho)$
$E[N_2] = (1 - \alpha)\rho/[(1 - \alpha\rho)(1 - \rho)]$

This situation also has the interesting result that

$E[N_1] + E[N_2] = \rho/(1 - \rho)$

The tradeoff behavior between the two classes is indicated in Figure 5-12 on the following page. The curves show the average system occupancy for each class C_1 and C_2 for different values of α. Notice that regardless of the value of α, $N_1 + N_2$ is a constant. Also notice the tradeoff between the two classes of customers as the traffic intensity increases.

Now consider the more general $M/G/1$ queue with multiple classes of customers, each with a different priority. For simplicity, assume a *nonpreemptive priority*. This means that a customer with a higher priority can move ahead of lower priority customers in the queue, but it cannot interrupt a customer who has entered the server. Also assume that the customers have priorities labeled $p = 1$, $2, \ldots, r$ in descending order of priority.

A customer with priority p enters the queue at time t_0 and begins service at time t_1. The time $t_1 - t_0$ is defined as the waiting time W_p. To analyze the queue,

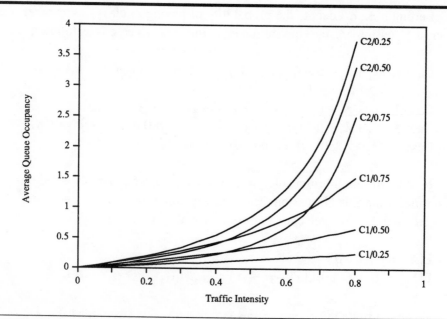

FIGURE 5-12   *M/M/*1 queue with two priority classes.

focus on W_p and its various components. These components include T_0, the time to complete the current service; the times T_k to service m_k customers with priority $k = 1, 2, \ldots, p$, that are already in the queue when the customer arrives; and times T'_k to service the customers with higher priorities that arrive during the waiting interval. Taking the expected values for all these quantities yields

$$E(W_p) = E(T_0) + \sum E(T_k) + \sum E(T'_k)$$

To evaluate $E(T_k)$, notice that there are, on average, $E(m_k)$ messages of priority k waiting in the queue. Because each of these requires a service time of $1/\mu_k$,

$$E(T_k) = E(m_k)/\mu_k$$

$E(m_k)$ is the difference between $E(n_k)$, the average number of customers waiting and in service, and the number in service. Assuming that the average arrival rate for customers with priority k is λ_k, the average number in service is $\rho_k = \lambda_k/\mu_k$. Applying Little's formula yields

$$E(n_k) = \lambda_k T = \lambda_k[E(W_k) + 1/\mu_k] = E(m_k) + \rho_k$$

From this, you obtain

$$E(m_k) = \lambda_k E(W_k)$$
$$E(T_k) = \rho_k E(W_k)$$

To determine the term $E(T_k)$, recall that this is the average time required to service customers of priority k higher than p that arrive during the average waiting time $E(W_p)$. Using the same technique as above,

$$E(T_k') = \rho_k E(W_p)$$

Putting these two new expressions back into the original equation for $E(W_p)$ yields

$$E(W_p) = E(T_0) + \sum \rho_k E(W_k) + E(W_p) \sum \rho_k$$

This equation can be solved recursively to yield the result that

$$E(W_p) = E(T_0)/[(1 - \beta_{p-1})(1 - \beta_p)]$$

where

$$\beta_p = \sum \rho_k$$

To determine $E(T_0)$, first consider a single priority queue. This is simply an $M/G/1$ queue. From the earlier discussion of the $M/G/1$ queue, the expected waiting time in this case is $(\lambda/2)E(\tau^2)/(1 - \rho)$. For this result to equal the result just derived, $E(T_0) = \lambda E(\tau^2)/2$. For multiple priority messages, the result is

$$E(T_0) = 1/2 \sum \lambda_k E(\tau_k^2)$$

To demonstrate the advantage of having different priorities, consider a communications system that has two types of messages, data messages and acknowledgment messages. Because the acknowledgment messages are generally shorter, they are given priority over the data message. Assume that the data messages arrive according to a Poisson distribution with parameter λ. Because every data message is acknowledged, the acknowledgment arrival rate is also λ. Assume that both message lengths are exponentially distributed, implying that the average service times are $1/\mu_d$ for the data and $1/\mu_a$ for the acknowledgment.

Because the message lengths are exponentially distributed, $\sigma_a^2 = 1/\mu_a^2$ and $\sigma_d^2 = 1/\mu_d^2$ and $E(\tau_a^2) = 2/\mu_a^2$ and $E(\tau_d^2) = 2/\mu_d^2$. The expected waiting times for the two message types are

$$E(W_a) = [(\rho_a/\mu_a) + (\rho_d/\mu_d)]/(1 - \rho_a)$$
$$E(W_d) = [(\rho_a/m_a) + (\rho_d/m_d)]/(1 - \rho_a)(1 - \rho_a - \rho_d)$$

Using real numbers, let the average data message length require one second to process ($1/\mu_d = 1$), the acknowledgment message require 0.1 seconds ($1/\mu_a = 0.1$), and the message arrival rate be one every two seconds ($\lambda_a = \lambda_d = 0.5$). Then $\rho_a = 0.05$, $\rho_d = 0.5$, and $\rho = 0.55$.

The average waiting time for the acknowledgment message is 0.53 seconds. Most of this time is spent waiting for the data message in the server when the acknowledgment arrives to complete service (because it is a nonpreemptive queue). The average waiting time for the data messages is $0.53/0.45 = 1.18$ seconds.

If there is no priority structure, both the acknowledgment messages and the data messages are served on a first-come, first-served basis. Both message types have the same average waiting time. In this case, the general $M/G/1$ formula applies. The average waiting time is

$$E(W) = 1/(1 - \rho) \sum (\rho_k/\mu_k), \rho = \sum \rho_k$$

Continuing with the numeric example, this average waiting time is $0.505/0.55 = 0.92$ seconds. By having a priority scheme, you can considerably reduce the waiting time for acknowledgment (0.92 to 0.53) with a small increase in the average waiting time for the data message (0.92 to 1.18).

QUEUEING NETWORKS

As noted at the beginning of the chapter, a data communications network is a complex system of servers and channels. This complexity can often be approximated by a single queue and studied and analyzed with the techniques just discussed. The more general case, however, is a network of queues. With increasing generality comes increasing complexity. In fact, explicit solutions are available for only two specific types of queueing networks. For other types of networks, approximation methods can be used to analyze and study.

The two types are called Jackson networks and Baskett, Chandy, Muntz, and Palacios or BCMP networks. Analysis of these networks is complex, requiring both mathematical rigor and substantial amounts of tedious calculations. The following discussion is limited to a presentation of the basic definitions and theorems along with an indication of the types of problems that can be addressed with the two networks.

Jackson Networks

Jackson networks are the simplest queueing networks. They consist of N servers with unbounded queues at each server. The advance of a customer from one server to another is represented by a Markov chain. There is no difference in the stochastic properties of the customers. The location of a customer at time T_{k+1} only depends on where the customer is at time T_k.

A Jackson network can be open or closed. An open network accepts customers from outside according to a Poisson process. It also has customers that leave the network, again according to a Poisson process. A closed system always has a constant number of customers. The network can be deterministic or stochastic.

A Jackson network has a stationary solution in product form. This solution provides the joint probabilities of the lengths of the various queues in the network. It is this property that makes the Jackson network useful in modeling and analyzing data communication systems.

To analyze a Jackson network, consider a queueing network that consists of N servers. The number of customers at station i is denoted by k_i. $k = (k_1, k_2, \ldots, k_N)$ is a state vector that describes the system. Changes of state are caused by arrivals of customers from outside the system, movements of customers from one station to another, and departures of customers from the system. This network is shown in Figure 5-13.

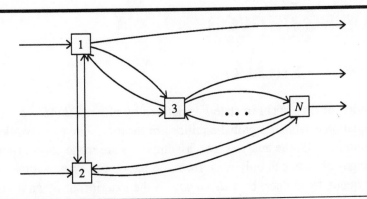

FIGURE 5-13   Jackson network.

Customers arriving from the exterior move towards the ith queue with constant probability p_{0i}. This is equivalent to a system in which each queue is fed from the exterior of the network following a Poisson process λp_{0i}.

Define p_{ij}, $i = 1, 2, \ldots, N$, $j = 1, 2, \ldots, N + 1$, as the constant probability that a customer completing service at server i goes to server j or the exterior for $j = N + 1$. The service times of the customers with the same server or different servers are independent random variables. The service time of server i when k_i customers are in the ith queue is an exponentially distributed random variable with parameter μ_i.

Using the same approach as used to analyze a single queue, consider a deterministic system that is observed over a defined time interval. Again let a and b be two times that define a time interval in which the state of the network is the same at the beginning as at the end. In this deterministic system the proportion of time spent in each state replaces the probabilities in a stochastic model. Let $D(k, k')$ be the number of transitions between two states k and k' during the interval. Because the state of the network is the same at the end of the interval as at the start, all transitions from k to k' must have a corresponding transition from k' to k during the interval. Therefore,

$$\sum D(k, k') = \sum D(k', k).$$

Now define $T(k)$ as the time spent in state k during the interval and $d(k, k')$ as the rate of transition from k to k'. This provides the relationship that

$$d(k, k') = D(k, k') / T(k).$$

Substituting this into the summation expression provides

$$\sum T(k)d(k, k') = \sum T(k)d(k, k')$$

or

$$\sum p(k)d(k, k') = \sum p(k)d(k, k')$$

if the fraction of time spent in state k is defined by $p(k) = T(k)/(b - a)$. The summation equation establishes global equilibrium for the queueing network.

To continue with the analysis, two assumptions are made concerning $d(k, k')$. First, changes of state can only arise from the passage of *one* customer at a time from one queue to another, by a *departure* to the exterior, or by an *arrival* from the exterior. For all other changes of state, $d(k, k') = 0$.

Second, the values of $d(k, k')$ assume local dependence. For the three non-zero cases of $d(k, k')$, its value is as follows:

$$d(k, k') = \begin{cases} p_{i,N+1}X_i(k_i + 1) & \text{Arrival from the exterior to queue } i \\ p_{0,i}X_0 & \text{Departure to the exterior from queue } i \\ p_{ij}X_i(k_i + 1) & \text{Customer leaves queue } j \text{ and goes to queue } i \end{cases}$$

The $p_{0,i}$ and p_{ij} are real and non-negative such that $\sum p_{0,i} = 1$, $p_{ii} = 0$, $\sum p_{ij} = 1$. The summation in the first case is for values of i from 1 to N. In the latter case, the summation is for values of j from 1 to $N + 1$. The X_i are real and non-negative such that $X_i(h) = 0$ if $h = 0$.

With these two assumptions, the solution for $p(k)$ is

$$p(k) = G^{-1} \prod_{i=1}^{N} \prod_{m=1}^{k_i} [e_i X_0 / X_i(m)]$$

G is a normalization constant that makes the sum of $p(k)$'s equal 1. The e_i are solutions to the system of equations:

$$e_i = p_{0,i} + \sum e_j p_{ji}, \quad i = 1, 2, \ldots, N$$

The result is very similar for a stochastic system. The result shown above, for a stochastic system, is denoted as the Jackson theorem. It is stated as follows.

For an open Jackson network, the stationary probability distribution, if it exists, is given by:

$$p(k) = p(\underline{0}) \prod_{i=1}^{N} \prod_{m=1}^{k_i} [\lambda e_i / \mu_i(m)]$$

where the e_i are the solution of the system of equations

$$e_i = p_{0,i} + \sum e_j p_{ji}, \quad i = 1, 2, \ldots, N$$

and where

$$1/p(\underline{0}) = \sum \prod_{i=1}^{N} \prod_{m=1}^{k_i} [\lambda e_i / \mu_i(m)]$$

Now consider a closed network. The difference here is that the number of customers is always the same. Customers can neither enter from nor leave to the exterior. If the number of customers is K, $\sum k = K$. The transition rate $d(k', k)$ is only non-zero for the case when a customer moves from queue j to queue i. For these cases, $d(k', k) = p_{ij} X_i(k_i + 1)$.

The solution of the equilibrium equations for this network is

$$p(k) = [G(K,N)^{-1}] \prod_{i=1}^{N} \prod_{m=1}^{k_i} [e_i/X_i(m)]$$

where $G(K,N)$ is a normalization constant and

$$e_i = \sum e_j p_{ji}, \, i = 1, 2, \ldots, N$$

Notice that this latter system of equations is not independent because of the constraint imposed on the sum of the p_{ji}. The solution is not unique.

Again, the result for a stochastic system is very similar. The Jackson theorem for a closed network is as follows.

For a closed Jackson network, the stationary probability distribution, if it exists, is given by:

$$p(k) = p(\underline{0}) \prod_{i=1}^{N} \prod_{m=1}^{k_i} [\lambda e_i/\mu_i(m)]$$

where the e_i are the solution of the system of equations

$$e_i = \prod e_j p_{ji}, \, i = 1, 2, \ldots, N$$

and where

$$1/p(\underline{0}) = \sum \prod_{i=1}^{N} \prod_{m=1}^{k_i} [\lambda e_i/\mu_i(m)]$$

In the case of a closed system, it is possible to use the solutions numerically, because there are a finite number of equations to solve. The first step is to calculate the normalization constant $G(K,N)$. A direct numerical approach, however, is impractical because of the large number of possible states. The number of possible states, for a system with K customers and N servers, is $(N + K - 1)!/(N - 1)!K!$. For example, if $N = 10$ and $K = 6$, the possible number of states is 5005. Algorithms exist that require on NK arithmetic operations when the X_i do not depend on the k_i. In the general case, the number of operations required is NK^2.

BCMP Networks

The Jackson network, while applicable in many situations, is limited to cases in which the arrival processes are all Poisson, the service times are all exponential, all service is first in, first out, and all customers are of the same class. A second type of network was introduced in the late 1970s which introduced different classes of customers and new service disciplines while still retaining a solution for the equilibrium state in product form.

This new network is denoted as a BCMP network, for Baskett, Chandy, Muntz, and Palacios. The BCMP network allows R classes of customers to circulate in the network. The probabilities of a step by a customer across a network are given by a Markov chain of transition probability:

$$P = \{p_{ir, jr}\} \text{ where } 0 \le i \le N, 1 \le j \le N + 1, 1 \le r, r'' \le R$$

The quantity $p_{ir, jr}$ expresses the probability that a customer in class r at station i goes to station j in class r'. $p_{ir, N+1jr'}$ is the probability that a customer in class r leaves the network at the end of his service in station i.

The BMCP network has four possible server disciplines. These are as follows:

- **Type 1**—The server is first in, first out. Each station has a single server with an exponential service time that is identical for all classes of customers.
- **Type 2**—This is a "time division" server. Each customer in the server receives $1/k$ seconds of service per second if k is the number of customers in the server at the time.
- **Type 3**—The number of servers at each station is sufficient so that at least one is always free. Every new customer entering the station begins service immediately. The service times can be different for different classes of customers.
- **Type 4**—The service discipline is strictly "last in, first served" with a single server. The arrival of a new customer at a station interrupts the service of the customer in the server at the time. The interrupted customer resumes service when the new customer leaves.

The BCMP theorem provides an expression for the equilibrium probabilities, which is only a function of the means of the service time distributions. The probabilities are in a form that allows the network to be studied station by station. As in the Jackson network solution, the principal difficulty is the calculation of the normalization constant.

Uses of Queueing Networks

A data communications network is a computer system in which numerous terminals and computers are interconnected. The individual user addresses the network, not any specific computer. The user is not concerned with the operation of the network. He only desires that the requested tasks be carried out correctly and that the results arrive with maximum speed.

Computer networks can be separated into two sections, the actual transport network and the computer transmitter-receivers. The transport network is a distributed system consisting of computers that route blocks of data to their destinations. The size of the blocks or packets is generally small, 256 bytes or less.

Two types of service are available for packet switching, transfer by datagram or by virtual circuit. Datagram service is a simple packet transmission service more or less elaborated by the addition of routing functions, stream control, and other ancillaries. The virtual circuit service involves calling and releasing procedures to establish and close connections. Buffers are reserved in the network nodes between two users. Each service method has advantages and disadvantages.

The pre-allocation of buffers involves underutilization of components but allows the circulation of packets in the network to be controlled more easily. Determination of the optimum number of buffers at each node is a problem that can be addressed by the use of queueing networks. You can also determine how the number of buffers affects the response time.

Allocation on demand provides a better utilization of buffers but increases the difficulty of dynamically controlling the streams. The tradeoff between pre-allocation and allocation on demand can also be studied with queueing networks.

SUMMARY

A *queueing system*, reduced to its simplest form, consists of a series of customers arriving at a group of identical *servers* and requesting service. If all servers are busy, the customers begin to form a *queue* to be served at some later time when server becomes free. The queueing system is characterized by three quantities: the input process, the service mechanism, and the queue discipline.

Little's formula states that the average number of customers in a queueing system is equal to the average arrival rate times the average time to service each customer. The formula applies to all types of queues.

Many queueing processes can be reduced to Markov chains. The behavior of the chain is generally a function of the traffic intensity ρ. ρ is the product of the average arrival rate and the average service time. If $\rho > 1$, the Markov chain is not ergodic and has no stable solution. The size of the queue grows without bound. If $\rho = 1$, the time needed to clear the queue approaches infinity. If $\rho < 1$, the Markov chain is ergodic and has a stable solution. In this case, you can determine the average length of the queue, the average service time, and other factors that describe the average behavior of the queue.

The simplest queueing system, using the Kendall notation, is the $M/M/1$ queue. In this queue, customers arrive at a single server at a Poisson rate of λ. The number of customers awaiting service can grow to infinity. The server processes each customer in a time that is exponentially distributed with an average value of $1/\mu$. In this queue, $\rho = \lambda/\mu$, the expected queue occupancy is $E(N) = \rho/(1 - \rho)$, and the average service time is $E(T) = 1/\mu(1 - \rho)$.

A more general queueing system is the $M/G/1$. In this system, no probability distribution is specified for the service time. The *Pollaczek-Khinchine formula* states that the average length of a $M/G/1$ queue $E(N) = (1/2(1 - \rho)[\sigma^2 + \rho(1 - \rho)\sigma^2]$ is the variance of the service time and ρ is the product of the average arrival rate and the average service time.

To better portray and understand data communications networks, queues can be combined into queueing networks. Only two types of queueing networks have solutions for the equilibrium state. These are *Jackson networks* and *Baskett, Chandy, Muntz, and Palacios* (BCMP) networks. These two types, however, have sufficient latitude to allow many type of data communications networks to be analyzed.

Queueing theory plays an important role in the quantitative understanding of data communications networks. It allows the concentration and buffering aspects of different network designs to be assessed before implementation. The application of queueing theory to real-world applications can become very complicated. Exact solutions are only available for certain special cases. Even in these cases, the calculation of the solution can be tedious and difficult.

SUGGESTED READING

In 1975, Kleinrock published *Queueing Systems*. It remains the most comprehensive treatment of queueing systems available. Cinlar's *Introduction to Stochastic Processes* provides a good discussion of the various Markov chains that are used in queueing analysis. *Introduction to Queueing Networks,* written by Gelenbe and Pujolle in France and translated by Nelson, is a good introductory text with discussion of many recent developments not included in Kleinrock. It includes algorithms for calculating the normalization constants for the solution of Jackson networks along with several example analyses of data communications networks.

6

ADDITIONAL TOPICS

FINITE STATE MACHINES

As shown in Chapter 3, a communication system can be readily reduced to six components, source, transmitter, channel, noise source, receiver, and destination. In a data communication system, the transmitter and receiver are typically computers. The computer itself consists of three primary components, the central processing unit, memory, and input-output devices. Continuing with the simplistic approach, the data communication computers each have a single input device and a single output device. This view of the system is shown in Figure 6-1.

The central processor units in the transmitter and receiver are brains of system. They are responsible for the individual arithmetical calculations and logical decisions that encode the source information prior to it being placed on a channel and decode the information when it is received. This encode/decode processing is limited by the amount of data that the unit can handle at any one time. Data that cannot be handled is stored temporarily in auxiliary memory or other type of system queue, as discussed in Chapter 5.

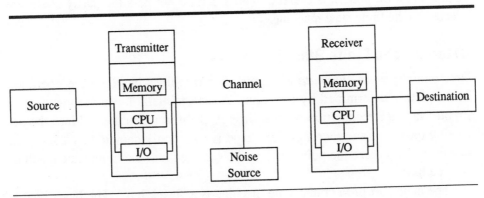

FIGURE 6-1 Communication system.

In Chapter 3, several different techniques were discussed for encoding and decoding data to detect and correct errors, compressing and decompressing the number of bits actually passed over the channel, and encrypting and decrypting the information. Other forms of encoding/decoding include message protocols, packetizing, and message routing. Although some simple algorithms were introduced with the techniques, actual implementation in a data communication system may require more details.

The concept of a *finite automaton* or a *finite state machine* is a useful tool for developing and implementing encoding/decoding algorithms. The finite state machine shares with the transmitter and receiver computer the property that its "central processor" has a fixed, finite capacity. Beyond this capacity, however, a finite state machine has no auxiliary memory. It receives input as a string of bits. It delivers no output at all, but it does indicate when the input string is considered acceptable.

On first glance, such a simple computational model might be too trivial to merit further investigation. After all, what is the use of a computer with no memory? The finite state machine is not really without memory; it simply has a memory capacity that is fixed "at the factory" and cannot be expanded. This fixed capacity can be quite large. Computers with large auxiliary memory units can be considered finite state machines, as long as expansion of the memory is not required.

The theory of finite automata and finite state machines is rich and elegant. Once understood, it is very applicable to that part of computer programming called lexical phrase analysis. This is the process of interpreting a string of characters and determining if they belong to an acceptable group of strings. A simple example of this are characters expressed in 8-bit words where the eighth bit is a parity bit. A finite state machine can analyze each word as it comes and determine if the 8-bit pattern is correct. Words that do not pass the parity check are rejected by the finite state machine.

Deterministic Finite State Machines

Deterministic finite automata are finite state machines in which the operation is completely determined by the input. A deterministic finite automaton is a simple language recognition device. Strings of information are fed into the device by means of an *input tape*. The tape is commonly depicted as a series of squares to emphasize the point that symbols are fed into the finite state machine one at a time.

The main part of the finite state machine is a "black box." The black box, at any specified instant in time, is in one of a finite number of distinct internal *states*. The box, also called the *finite control*, can sense the symbol that is written on the tape by means of a moveable *reading head*. Initially, the reading head is placed at the leftmost square of the tape, and the finite control is set in a designated *initial state*. Figure 6-2 depicts a finite state machine along with its three components.

At regular intervals, the finite state machine reads one symbol from the input tape and then enters a new state that depends only on the current state and the symbol just read (i.e., the same as a Markov chain). After reading the input symbol, the reading head moves one square to the right to prepare to read the next symbol. The process repeats until the reading head reaches the end of the input string.

When the end of the tape is reached, the finite state machine indicates whether or not the string is an approved string. This is indicated by the *final state* of the black box. The *language accepted* by the finite state machine is the set of strings it accepts. This explanation can be reduced to the following mathematical essentials.

A deterministic finite state machine is a quintuple $M = (K, \Sigma, \delta, s, F)$ where

K is a finite set of *states*,
Σ is an alphabet of input symbols,
$s \in K$ is the *initial state*
$F \subseteq K$ is the set of *final states*,

and δ, the *transition function*, is the function from $K \times \Sigma$ to K.

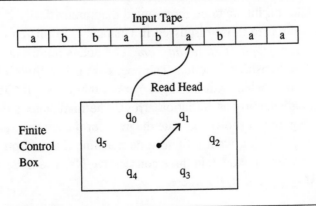

FIGURE 6-2   Finite state machine.

The rules that govern which state the finite state machine goes into are encoded in the transition function. If M is in state $q \in K$ and the symbol read from the input tape is $\sigma \in \Sigma$, $\delta(q, \sigma) \in K$ is the uniquely determined state to which M passes.

Now that the formal definition is established, the actual computation of a finite state machine on an input string must be developed in mathematical terms. This will be a sequence of configurations that represent the status of the finite control, reading head, and input tape as successive moments. Because a finite state machine is not allowed to move the reading head backward, the portion of the string to the left of the reading head cannot influence the future operation of the finite state machine. The configuration is therefore determined by the current state and the unread part of the string still to be processed. The configuration of a deterministic finite state machine $(K, \Sigma, \delta, s, F)$ is any element of $K \times \Sigma^*$. For example, the configuration shown in Figure 6-2 is $(q_1, abaa)$.

To demonstrate these concepts, consider the simple finite state machine M consisting of two states (q_0, q_1) and two alphabet characters (a, b). The starting state is q_0. The transition function δ is as follows:

q	σ	$\delta(q, \sigma)$
q_0	a	q_0
q_0	b	q_1
q_1	a	q_1
q_1	b	q_0

The *language accepted by* M is denoted as $L(M)$. In this case, $L(M)$ is the set of all strings $\{a, b\}$ that have an even number of b's in the string. The finite state machine essentially counts the b's modulo 2. The string is accepted if the machine is in state q_0 at the end of the string.

A finite state machine can be represented diagrammatically by a labeled directed graph, similar to those discussed in Chapter 4. In this case, the graph is called a *transition graph* or *state diagram*. The nodes represent states and the arcs represent the transition function. The nodes are generally labeled with their state. The arcs are labeled with the input symbol that causes the transition. The initial state is indicated by an initiation arrow. The final state is denoted with a double circle. Figure 6-3 shows the state diagram for the above example.

Now assume that you want a finite state machine that accepts the language $L(M)$ if the word does not contain three consecutive b's. The finite state machine is defined as $M = (K, \Sigma, \delta, s, F)$ where

$K = \{q_0, q_1, q_2, q_3\}$
$\Sigma = \{a, b\}$
$s = q_0$
$F = \{q_0, q_1, q_2\}$

δ is as follows:

q	σ	$\delta(q, \sigma)$
q_0	a	q_0
q_0	b	q_1
q_1	a	q_0
q_1	b	q_2
q_2	a	q_0
q_2	b	q_3
q_3	a	q_3
q_3	b	q_3

The state diagram is shown in Figure 6-4. Notice that after state q_3 is reached, M remains in the state regardless of the symbols in the rest of the input string. State q_3 is said to be a *dead state*. If the machine reaches state q_3, it is said to be *trapped*, because no further output will allow it to escape from this state.

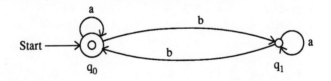

FIGURE 6-3 State diagram.

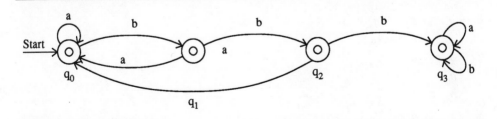

FIGURE 6-4 State diagram.

Nondeterministic Finite State Machines

The difference between a deterministic finite state machine and a nondeterministic one is that in the latter case, the machine can change states in a way that is only partially determined by the current state and the input symbol. Instead of having a single, deterministic result from a given symbol/state combination, a nondeterministic finite state machine can move into one of several possible states. The choice of which state the model goes into is not determined by anything in the model. The choice is not, however, unlimited. Only those next states that are legitimate transitions from the current state and input symbol can be chosen.

Nondeterminism is not a feature normally associated with computers, but it naturally arises as an extension of the behavior of deterministic finite state machines. An example would be deciding which path a message will take when both paths are determined to have the same cost. The state of the network will change, but the end result does not.

To illustrate the differences between a deterministic and nondeterministic finite state machine, consider a machine that accepts character strings which only contain sequences $\{ab\}$ or $\{aba\}$. The state diagram is shown in Figure 6-5. The deterministic finite state machine contains five different states and is defined as $M = (K, \Sigma, \delta, s, F)$ where

$$K = \{q_0, q_1, q_2, q_3, q_3\}$$
$$\Sigma = \{a, b\}$$
$$s = q_0$$
$$F = \{q_2, q_3\}$$

δ is as follows:

q	σ	$\delta(q, \sigma)$
q_0	a	q_1
q_0	b	q_4
q_1	a	q_4
q_1	b	q_2
q_2	a	q_3
q_2	b	q_4
q_3	a	q_1
q_3	b	q_2
q_4	a	q_4
q_4	b	q_4

Even with the diagram, it is not easy to ascertain that a deterministic finite state machine is depicted. Careful checking indicates that there are only two arrows leaving each node, one labeled a and one labeled b. A much simpler depiction, and much simpler machine, is possible if two outcomes are possible with one combination of symbol and machine state. Consider the diagram shown in Figure 6-6.

When the machine is in state q_1 and the input symbol is b, there are two possible next states, q_0 and q_2. Therefore the diagram is not a deterministic finite state machine. It does, however, accept the same sequences of characters that are accepted by the deterministic finite state machine. Also notice that from q_0, there is no state to be entered when the input is b. Similarly, there is no b coming out of state q_2. This is another property of a nondeterministic finite state machine, that there may be some combinations of states and input symbols where no move is possible.

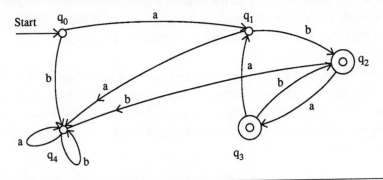

FIGURE 6-5 State diagram—deterministic finite state machine.

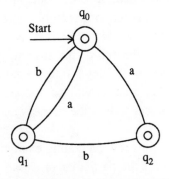

FIGURE 6-6 State diagram—nondeterministic finite state machine.

The formal definition for a deterministic finite state machine is as follows:

A nondeterministic finite state machine is a quintuple $M = (K, \Sigma, \Delta, s, F)$ where

> K is a finite set of *states*,
> Σ is an alphabet of input symbols,
> $s \in K$ is the *initial state*
> $F \subseteq K$ is the set of *final states*,

and Δ, the *transition relation*, is the function from $K \times \Sigma^* \times K$.

The significance of the triple (q, u, p) being in Δ is that M, when in state q, may consume a string u from the input string and enter state p. In other words, $(q, u, p) \in \Delta$ if and only if the arrow labeled u goes from node q to node p in the state diagram. Each triple $(q, u, p) \in \Delta$ is called a *transition* of M. In keeping with the idea that M is a finite machine, Δ must be a finite set even though $K \times \Sigma^* \times K$ is an infinite set.

By definition, two finite state machines are said to be equivalent if they accept the same language, even though they may use different methods. Much of the power of nondeterministic finite state machines is drawn from the fact that for each nondeterministic, there exists an equivalent deterministic finite state machine.

Using Finite State Machines

Finite state machines are useful analogies when developing several different kinds of programs for communication. The concept of a finite state machine is particularly useful in coding aspects or protocols. In coding, the finite state machine receives a steady stream of bits. The bits move the finite state machine from one state to another. At the end of the stream, the stream is judged to be either a legitimate character or an illegal one. Legal characters are passed on. Protocol handlers are another area in which finite state machine representation provides a useful tool to understanding the process and implementing the actual computer code.

In the following paragraphs, several coding examples from Chapter 3 will be discussed. A state diagram for the particular process will be developed for each example. A simple implementation of a routing scheme is also shown.

Error Checking Finite State Machines

Parity checking is a common scheme used to detect single bit errors in data blocks of fixed length. A word with a parity bit added corresponds to encoding scheme with a Hamming distance of 2. A finite state machine that detects the parity of a data block will accept, in this case, blocks with even parity. Blocks with odd parity are rejected. Even parity implies that the total number of 1's in the block is even.

Using the same notation as before, the finite state machine is $M = (K, \Sigma, \delta, s, F)$ where

$K = \{\text{even, odd}\}$
$\Sigma = \{0, 1\}$
$s = \text{even (0 is considered an even number)}$
$F = \{\text{even}\}$

δ is as follows:

q	σ	$\delta(q, \sigma)$
even	0	even
even	1	odd
odd	0	odd
odd	1	even

The state diagram for the parity detector finite state machine is shown in Figure 6-7. Notice that the operation of the machine is not dependent on the number of bits in the block or the location of the parity bit. The machine is such that it changes state if a 1 is received. The state remains unchanged if a 0 is received.

To operate the machine, let the input tape be 10011010. When the finite state machine read head moves across the tape, the states are as shown on the following page.

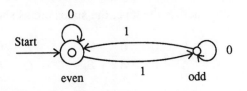

FIGURE 6-7 Parity detector finite state machine.

	1	0	0	1	1	0	1	0
New State	Even	Odd	Odd	Odd	Even	Odd	Odd	Even	Even

Since the machine is in the even state when the tape is finished reading, the word 10011010 is accepted.

For a slightly more complicated example, consider a coding scheme where each bit is repeated twice. To ensure that the data stream is correct, the code must consist of consecutive pairs. Otherwise a transmission has had an error. Also, the received word must contain an even number of bits to ensure both bits were received.

Using the same notation as before, the finite state machine is $M = (K, \Sigma, \delta, s, F)$ where

$K = \{A, B, C, D\}$
$\Sigma = \{0, 1\}$
$s = A$
$F = \{A\}$

δ is as follows:

q	σ	$\delta(q, \sigma)$
A	0	B
A	1	C
B	0	A
B	1	D
C	1	A
C	0	D
D	0	D
D	1	D

The state diagram for the repeating bit detector finite state machine is shown in Figure 6-8. Again, the operation of the machine is not dependent on the number of bits in the block. State D is a dead state.

To operate the machine, let the input tape be 11001110. When the finite state machine read head moves across the tape, the states are as shown below.

	1	1	0	0	0	1	1	0
New State	A	C	A	B	A	B	D	D	D

Once the machine reaches state D, it stays there. Because the machine does not finish in state A, the word is not accepted.

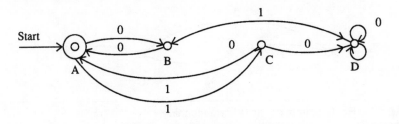

FIGURE 6-8 Repeated bit error detector finite state machine.

Route Determiner Finite State Machine

Consider a communications processor that routes messages over various lines depending on the header address. Once the header is read and judged to be legitimate, the data is allowed to pass through. If the header is not correct, the message is stopped.

This process can be portrayed by a finite state machine. In the example system, the header address consists of the first three bits of the signal. In this particular example, 010 and 011 are acceptable addresses. Messages for all other addresses are terminated. The finite state machine to model this process is $M = (K, \Sigma, \delta, s, F)$ where

$K = \{A, B, C, D\}$
$\Sigma = \{0, 1\}$
$s = A$
$F = \{D\}$

δ is as follows:

q	σ	$\delta(q, \sigma)$
A	0	C
A	1	B
B	0	B
B	1	B
C	1	D
C	0	B
D	0	D
D	1	D

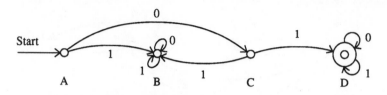

FIGURE 6-9   Route determiner finite state machine.

The state diagram is shown in Figure 6-9. In the finite state machine, there are two dead states, *B* and *D*. If the message header is such that it ends in *D*, the address is legitimate and the message is forwarded. Illegitimate headers end up in state *B*. Although this is a simple system, it could easily be extended to a series of finite state machines, with each one forwarding the data for a specific destination.

ADVANCED CODING TECHNIQUES

Chapter 3 introduced the subject of coding to compress the length of the message or to provide error detection and error correction. In recent years, two new coding techniques have emerged that are becoming widely used, especially as methods are sought for reliably transmitting data at 9600 bits per second over ordinary dial-up telephone lines.

The two coding techniques are called *cyclic redundant coding* (CRC) and *trellis coding*. Cyclic redundant coding is a form of block coding. Trellis coding is based on the technique of convolutional codes. The purpose of this section is to introduce the techniques and provide a basic understanding of their abilities.

Cyclic Redundant Codes

Cyclic redundant codes are derived from the concepts of block coding. The technique is memoryless and can be implemented with combinational logic. The codes are so named because the encoding process involves shifting the bits in a message through a register one bit at a time. The algebraic properties of the codes are such that error detection is relatively simple to implement.

A CRC is generated when the transmitter produces a bit pattern called a *frame check sequence* (sometimes called a *block check sequence*). The combined contents of the frame and the frame check sequence is exactly divisible by some predetermined number with no remainder. (Alternately, the division can result in a predetermined remainder.) If error occurs in the frame during its passage over the communication channel, the receiver's division will yield a non-zero remainder. A CRC detects several types of errors, including:

1. All single-bit errors.
2. All double-bit errors if the divisor is at least three terms.
3. Any odd number of errors if the divisor contains a factor $(x + 1)$.
4. Any error in which the length of the error (an error burst) is less than the length of the frame check sequence.
5. Most errors with larger bursts.

The generation and checking of the frame check sequence is best expressed with algebraic notation. The modulo 2 divisor is called a *generator polynomial*. The divisor is actually one bit longer than the frame check sequence. Both high-order and low-order bits of the divisor must have a value of 1. For example, the generator polynomial for the bit sequence 10110001 is represented by the polynomial:

$$f(x) = x^7 + x^5 + x^4 + 1$$

The process of generating a CRC is as follows:

1. The frame contents are appended by a set of 0's equal in number to the frame check sequence.
2. The new value is divided modulo 2 by the generator polynomial (which contains one more digit than the frame check sequence and has the high-order and low-order bits equal to 1).
3. Each division is carried out in the conventional manner except that the subtraction is done modulo 2. This process is identical to the logical operation "exclusive or".
4. The answer provides a quotient, which is discarded, and a remainder, which becomes the frame check sequence field. The field is appended to the original frame and transmitted.
5. At the receiving end, the receiver performs the same division on the frame contents and the frame check sequence field. Because the frame check sequence (the remainder) replaced the original zeros, the remainder should be zero. A non-zero remainder indicates a transmission error.

To illustrate the CRC process, assume that the frame contents are 111001, and the generating polynomial is 11001 ($x^4 + x^3 + 1$). When four 0's are appended to the frame, the result is 1100010000.

The division process is as follows

```
              10001  —quotient ignored
   11001   ⌐110001000
              11001
              11000
              11001
              0001   —remainder becomes frame sequence check
```

The resulting transmitted value is then 110010001.

Two commonly used generating polynomials are CRC-16 ($x^{16} + x^{15} + x^2 + -11000000000000101$) and CRC-CCITT ($x^{16} + x^{12} + x^5 + 1 - 10001000000100001$). Both schemes detect errors of burst up to 16 bits in length. CRC-CCITT detects 99 percent of error bursts greater than 12 bits while CRC-16 detects 99 percent of error bursts longer than 16 bits. Notice, however, that CRC techniques only detect errors. They do not correct errors.

Trellis Coding

Trellis coding is a form of convolutional coding. A convolutional encoder is similar in many respects to a Hamming encoder, especially Hamming encoders with large block sizes. Both encoders use memory. Both accept a block of k-bit information blocks and produce n-bit symbol blocks. In a Hamming encoder, each block is independent of other blocks. In a convolutional encoder, the code word value depends on the m previous code words. The resulting encoded value is called an (n, m, k) convolutional code. Convolutional encoders are implemented with sequential logic.

A simple convolutional encoder is depicted in Figure 6-10. As can be seen, because the encoder is a sequential process, it is readily depicted with a state diagram to form a quasi finite state machine. A stream of information bits enters the machine at S_0. The numbers to the left of the slash are the information bits. The numbers to the right are the bits for the code word. The k bits of the information block are read one at a time, moving through the machine and creating the n bit code word. When the last non-zero bit is read, the machine continues to operate until it returns to S_0, adding 0's to the code word as it goes.

Trellis coding possesses a sufficient Hamming distance to correct as well as detect errors. It is a member of a new family of codes known as forward error correcting. The idea behind trellis coding is that the transmission signal always starts at a known value that is confined within certain limits, the letters of the alphabet for instance. In the trellis method, the signal is allowed to assume only

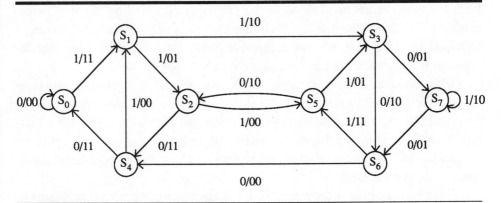

FIGURE 6-10 Convolutional encoder.

certain states when on the communication channel. Also, the bits are interpreted such that only certain states are allowed to exist from previous states.

This means the transmitter accepts a series of bits and develops additional yet restricted bit patterns (or states). The previous bit pattern is only allowed to assume certain other patterns. Other states are invalid and never transmitted.

The transmitter and receiver are programmed to understand the allowable states and the permissible state transitions. If the receiver receives states and state transitions that differ (because of errors) from the allowable transition, an error is detected. This process is readily depicted by a finite state machine.

Trellis coding, however, does more than just detect the error. Because the transmitter and receiver know the transmission states and permissible transitions, the receiver analyzes the received signal and makes a "best guess" as to what state the signal should assume. It uses a path history to reconstruct damaged bits.

Trellis coding and other forward error correcting codes have the potential to instigate a major revision to data communication software and hardware. Trellis coded modulation has been shown to reduce error rates by three orders of magnitude. As trellis coding becomes more pervasive, data link controls and online protocols will undergo significant changes.

SUMMARY

The *finite state machine* consists of the *finite controller*, *read head*, and *input tape*. The read head passes over the input tape one symbol at a time. Depending on the symbol, the finite controller may or may not change state. If, at the end of the tape, the finite controller is in an *acceptable* state, the string of symbols read from the tape are assumed to be in the *language* accepted by the finite state machine. The finite state machine is defined by a set of possible states, an input alphabet, an initial state, a set of acceptable final states, and a transition that determines what the next state is for a given state and input symbol.

A *deterministic* finite state machine has one and only one possible state transition associated with each state/input symbol combination. A *nondeterministic* finite state machine may transition to more than one state for a given input symbol. Two finite state machines that accept the same language are said to be *equivalent*. Every nondeterministic finite state machine has an equivalent deterministic finite state machine.

Finite state machines provide a useful analogy for constructing programs to encode and decode bit streams. The state diagrams associated with finite state machines are useful tools for understanding the process and for building algorithms to implement the procedures.

Cyclic redundant coding is an extension of blocking coding. It is particularly useful for detecting error bursts and is relatively easy to implement. *Trellis coding* is a form of a convolutional code. A recent innovation, it provides significant reduction in errors by using previously received information to make a "best guess" when an error is detected.

SUGGESTED READING

The subject of finite state machines and finite automata has not produced a large number of books. It is often discussed as a chapter in books on computational theory, such as *Elements of the Theory of Computation* by Lewis and Papadimitriou. The classical paper on finite automata, by Rabin and Scott, appeared in the *IBM Journal of Research and Development* in 1959.

Viterbi discusses some of the early work on trellis coding in his 1967 paper, published in the *IEEE Transaction on Information Theory*. Payton and Quereshi explain practical applications of trellis coding in their paper in the May 1985 issue of *Data Communications*.

BIBLIOGRAPHY

Berge, Claude, *Graphs*, 2nd edition, New York, NY, North Holland, sole distributors for the U.S.A. and Canada, Elsevier Science Publishing Company, 1985.

Berlekamp, E. R., *Algebraic Coding Theory*, New York, NY, McGraw Hill, 1980.

Bertsekas, Dimitri, Robert Gallager, *Data Networks*, Englewood Cliffs, NJ, Prentice Hall, 1986.

Black, Uyless, *Data Networks: Concepts, Theory, and Practice*, Englewood Cliffs, NJ, Prentice Hall, 1989.

Black, Uyless, *Computer Networks: Products, Standards, and Interfaces*, Englewood Cliffs, NJ, Prentice Hall, 1987.

Cinlar, Erhan, *Introduction to Stochastic Process*, Englewood Cliffs, NJ, Prentice Hall, 1975.

Cooper, Robert B., *Introduction to Queueing Theory*, New York, NY, Macmillan Company, 1972.

Davies, D. W., D. L. A. Barber, W. L. Price, C. M. Solomonides, *Computer Networks and Their Protocols*, New York, NY, John Wiley, 1979.

Diffie, Whitfield, Martin E. Hellman, "New Directions in Cryptography," *IEEE Transactions on Information Theory*, Vol. IT-22, No. 6, pp. 644–654, November 1976.

Ellis, Robert L., *Designing Data Networks*, Englewood Cliffs, NJ, Prentice Hall, 1987.

Feller, William, *An Introduction to Probability Theory and Statistics*, Vol. I, 3rd edition, New York, NY, John Wiley, 1968.

Feller, William, *An Introduction to Probability Theory and Statistics*, Vol. II, 2nd edition, New York, NY, John Wiley, 1971.

Ford, L. R., D. R. Fulkerson, *Flows in Networks*, Princeton, NJ, Princeton University Press, 1962.

Gallager, Robert G., *Information Theory and Reliable Communication,* New York, NY, John Wiley, 1968.

Gelenbe, E., G. Pujolle, J. C. C. Nelson, *Introduction to Queueing Networks,* New York, NY, John Wiley, 1987.

Hamming, Richard W., *Coding and Information Theory,* Second Edition, Englewood Cliffs, NJ, Prentice Hall, 1986.

Hamming, Richard W., "Error Detecting and Error Correcting Codes," *Bell Systems Technical Journal,* Vol. 29, pp. 147–160, April 1950.

Hayes, Jeremiah F., *Modeling and Analysis of Computer Communications Networks,* New York, NY, Plenum Press, 1984. Computer networks, mathematical models.

Huffman, David A., "A Method for the Construction of Minimum-Redundancy Codes," *Proceedings of the IRE,* Vol. 40, pp. 1098–1101, September 1952.

Jensen, Paul A., J. Wesley Barnes, *Network Flow Programming,* New York, NY, John Wiley, 1981.

Jensen, Randall W., Bruce O. Watkins, *Network Analysis: Theory and Computer Methods,* Englewood Cliffs, NJ, Prentice Hall, 1974.

Kleinrock, Leonard, *Queueing Systems,* New York, NY, John Wiley, 1975.

Lewis, Harry R., Christos H. Papadimitriou, *Elements of the Theory of Computation,* Englewood Cliffs, NJ, Prentice Hall, 1981.

MacWilliams, F. J., N. J. A. Sloan, *The Theory of Error Correcting Codes,* North Holland Publishing Company, New York, NY, 1978.

Minieka, Edward, *Optimization Algorithms for Networks and Graphs,* New York, NY, Marcel Dekker Company, 1978.

Payton, John, Shahid Quereshi, "Trellis Encoding: What It Is and How It Effects Data Transmission," *Data Communications,* May 1985.

Pless, Vera, *Introduction to the Theory of Error Correcting Codes,* New York, NY, John Wiley, 1982.

Rabin, M. O., D. Scott, "Finite Automata and their Decision Problems," *IBM Journal of Research and Development,* Vol. 3, pp. 114–125, 1959.

Schwartz, Mischa, *Computer Communications Network Design and Analysis,* Englewood Cliffs, NJ, Prentice Hall, 1977.

Shannon, Claude E., "A Mathematical Theory of Communications, Part 1," *Bell Systems Technical Journal,* Vol. 27, pp. 379–423, July 1948.

Shannon, Claude E., "A Mathematical Theory of Communications, Part 2," *Bell Systems Technical Journal,* Vol. 27, pp. 623–656, October 1948.

Smith, David K., *Network Optimisation Practices: A Computational Guide,* New York, NY, John Wiley, 1982.

Stallings, William, *Data and Computer Communications,* New York, NY, Macmillan, 1985.

Stallings, William, *Data and Computer Communications*, 2nd edition, New York, NY, Macmillan, 1988.

Tanenbaum, Andrew S., *Computer Networks*, Englewood Cliffs, NJ, Prentice Hall, 1981.

Viterbi, A. J., "Error Bound for Convolutional Codes and an Asymptotically Optimum Decoding Algorithm," *IEEE Transactions on Information Theory*, Vol. IT-13, No. 2, April 1967.

Welch, Terry A., "A Technique for High-Performance Data Compression," *Computer*, June 1984.

Wilson, Robin J., *Introduction to Graph Theory*, New York, NY, Longman, 1985.

Ziv, Jacob, Abraham Lempel, "A Universal Algorithm for Sequential Data Compression," *IEEE Transactions on Information Theory*, Vol. IT-23, No. 3, pp. 337–343, May 1977.

INDEX

Numbers in italics denote figures and/or tables.